Contents

INTRODUCTION

Most of us are not born gardeners; parents and background seem to contribute little to what can become a future and often passionate pursuit. In fact, the majority of people develop no interest in the subject until faced with their first garden plot. Of course, there are exceptions, particularly among those gardeners who inherit skills and even established gardens from their parents. Christopher Lloyd, one of the greatest modern gardeners, was born with a metaphorical 'silver trowel' in his hands. He continues to garden at Great Dixter (see pp. 96-9) where he was brought up and influenced by his parents. His writings, which are widely respected and enjoyed, describe his day-to-day gardening activities and the immense pleasure he gets from them. In fact some of the greatest gardens have been owned and administered by the same family over several generations. At Tresco Abbey in the Isles of Scilly five generations of the Dorrien-Smith family have planted and cherished the gardens; at Nymans and at Leonards Lee, both in Sussex, there has been similar continuity.

As Jane Brown elaborates in *The English Garden in Our Time* recent garden history is, in the main, the story of the making of great gardens by individual gardeners and designers rather than symptomatic of a style or a 'movement'. What she writes about England is also true of America and Europe. She traces the emergence of an individual's own particular style from the story of their life and education. Lawrence Johnston's development of the garden at Hidcote before the 1914-18 war must have been inspired by his travels in Italy and France as a young man but also reflects the fashion of the time for creating an architectural framework as a background to an assembly of hardy plants. Developing an awareness and appreciation of historical and contemporary 'styles' contributes to a gardener's own development and is not just an aesthetic exercise; it is a question of interpreting a garden setting and then handling and arranging plants suitably. Each of us as gardeners will 'develop' our own style; visiting great or small gardens will not result in slavish copying but, rather, leads to an increased ability to adapt to an individual situation. Often it may be a single area of a great garden that inspires, or just some very simple plant association – colour, texture, shape or relative scale. Appropriate garden features and planting are achieved by developing a strong visual sense and by understanding a plant's requirements.

Gardening as an art form differs from all others. In gardening, man provides designs, implements the layout and ensures the garden's maintenance. Yet nature provides the other essential ingredients: growing and living plants which, given sufficient time, bring a plan, on whatever scale, to its fulfilment. At different periods of history, gardening philosophy and fashion have swung between two extremes. One, where art and contrivance are all important and nature's part is relegated to providing the materials for clipped or pleached hedges and topiary shapes, emphasizes the value of artificial effects at the expense of more natural ones (see particularly *The Patterned Garden* pp. 100-29). The opposite view

LEFT Francis Cabot's garden at La Malbaie, north of Quebec, has a classic axial design and takes full advantage of vistas to forest, mountains and water. It is a garden of compartments where formal perennial border schemes, in isolated colour sequences, swiftly change to scenes with woodland canopies sheltering naturalized carpets of Asiatic primulas or native flora. The garden layout is complicated by changes of level which, all through the garden, are adjusted by broad steps. The dramatic descending cascades, their banks uncluttered by planting, are framed by woodland and narrow in width as they fall; they are reminiscent of those, in tamer English landscapes, designed by

Harold Peto at Buscot House and more recently by Sir Geoffrey Jellicoe.

RIGHT At Cobblers in Sussex a light-reflecting lily-pool surrounded by luxuriant planting lies on the south slope of the garden. Waterside perennials with strong foliage shapes contrast with thrusting iris leaves and graceful drooping grasses. In season primulas and the American skunk cabbage, *Lysichiton americanum*, contribute flower and colour. The success of this sort of naturalistic gardening lies in making plants seem at home in their setting.

RIGHT Ryan Gainey's garden in Atlanta, Georgia, is backed by woods of native American beech (*Fagus grandiflora*) and dogwood (*Cornus florida*). Four identical sections are separated by straight pathways which lead to a central box-edged circle, the design accentuated by the inner ring of paving laid like radiating wheel spokes. Four standard *Hydrangea paniculata* 'Grandiflora' give height above beds of blue-flowered iris, violas and spring forget-me-nots.

FAR RIGHT Raised stone-edged beds in the old cloisters of this Somerset garden are thickly planted to give interest all through the year. Golden and green-leaved yews are architectural; winter-flowering prunus, *Magnolia* × *soulangiana* and red-berried elder (*Sambucus racemosa* 'Plumosa Aurea'), give height against the walls. A standard wisteria, underplanted with blue-flowered *Campanula garganica*, makes a focal point in the central bed, the meeting place of the four paths.

stresses the importance of a naturalistic impression where art is employed to deceive the eye so that a garden appears to imitate nature (see *The More Natural Garden* pp. 130-57).

The 18th-century English landscape became the extreme example of nature's apparent triumph over art. The park was refashioned and the land contoured to include natural-looking groves of trees and expanses of reflecting water. In grand landscapes a ha-ha, concealed between the garden and parkland, while allowing an uninterrupted view outwards, made a barrier against animals without making an obvious division between the two areas. Adopted by pioneers of the English landscape school in the 18th century, it became a symbol of unity between garden and countryside, an essential tool in the development of garden 'naturalism'. The landscape became England's greatest artistic

contribution to western civilization. Its implications were immense and it represented a whole philosophy, intimately connected with literature and painting, often allegorical in meaning and classical in derivation. Supreme examples of its style remain part of England's heritage.

The modern upkeep and maintenance of mansions surrounded by 'Capability' Brown or Repton parkland pose problems which require far-seeing dedication. The great 18th-century landscapers planned for future generations, and the two-hundred-year-old trees, the backbone of the designs, are now reaching the end of a natural span and must be felled and replaced. This is gardening on a grand scale where planting is for posterity rather than for immediate enjoyment. As fashions changed, more intimate gardens in a variety of styles were created round a mansion by successive

generations. Today, their heirs have to adapt these often labour-intensive schemes to modern methods. The future of many of our great gardens depends on a new owner's interest and dedication. Others, of course, are looked after by the National Trust (in the United Kingdom) and similar bodies in some European countries and North America, usually a form of charitable trust which assures their future.

Many of the best garden writers, those individuals who have influenced garden style in the last hundred years, speak from personal experience. Gertrude Jekyll at Munstead Wood, Vita Sackville-West at Sissinghurst, Margery Fish at East Lambrook, and Christopher Lloyd at Great Dixter all make their own gardens the subject of their writing. In America, Elizabeth Lawrence (who died in 1985) wrote about her own garden in Raleigh, North Caro-

lina: the result is an extraordinary evocation of the actual joy of handling plants and working the soil. Hugh Johnson, wine expert and writer on trees, wrote *The Principles of Gardening* as he made his own garden at Saling Hall in Essex.

Some have come to gardening through painting. Gertrude Jekyll was first trained as an artist and she applied the rules of pictorial composition and colour theory to her garden views. Monet, rather differently, planted his garden at Giverny in order to paint it later. John Hubbard at Chilcombe (see p. 206) has a more abstract style but his sense of colour rhythms clearly affects his own gardening patterns.

Sometimes garden designers have made their gardens a particular artistic quest, or have been influenced by literary or historical traditions. The sculptor Ian Hamilton Finlay made a garden in

LEFT At Giverny (see pp. 184-5) Monet used very simple cottage-garden flowers, planted in great profusion to provide subjects for his paintings. He liked to have some flower colour all through the year; old fashioned columbines and pink-flowered *Oxalis* were encouraged to seed through the beds between seasonal drifts of perennials and annuals.

RIGHT In the 1970s, in a valley under the Luberon hills in Provence, the late Mr Roderick Cameron created a new garden with formal planting near the house, the style gradually becoming more relaxed as paths ran along the slopes in the woodland. Beside the walls, built of local stone, pyramids of box are used as architectural accents in patterned box-edged beds set in pale gravel. Few bright colours are used in this garden; instead subtle shades and textures of green foliage harmonize in areas of sun and shade. Looking past the house, a smooth lawn appears as a pool of sunlight and elegant stone urns frame a vista into the orchards beyond the garden.

Scotland where his own works often have allegorical meanings; features in the 16th-century villa gardens at Castello outside Florence glorified the Medici family and scenes from Ovid's *Metamorphoses* were typified by statues representing the Apennines as human figures. Garden mazes, with themes stolen from Greek mythology or Christian teaching, traditionally illustrate man's quest for salvation; at Stourhead the garden is related to Virgil's journey through the underworld. Sir Geoffrey Jellicoe's modern designs for Sutton Place tried to encapsulate the whole history of western civilization. Painting, philosophy, literature and religion will all influence man's individual interpretation of the 'genius of the place'.

As Miss Jekyll says in her introduction to *Wood and Garden*, 'the scope of practical gardening covers a range of horticultural practice wide enough to give play to every variety of human taste. Some find their greatest pleasure in collecting as large a number as possible of all sorts of plants from all sources, others in collecting them themselves in their foreign homes, others in making rock gardens, or ferneries or peat gardens, or bog gardens, or gardens for conifers or for flowering shrubs, or special gardens of plants and trees with variegated or coloured leaves, or in the cultivation of some particular race or family of plants. Others may best like wide lawns with large trees or wild gardening, or quite a formal garden, with trim hedge and walk and terrace, and brilliant parterre, or a combination of several ways of gardening. All are right and reasonable and enjoyable to their owners, and in some way or degree helpful to others.'

Within Miss Jekyll's brief we must include gardens which, in a strict historical sense, are restored or redesigned to surround and complement a house of a set period. The Marchioness of Salisbury has restored the garden at 16th-century Cranborne Manor in Dorset (see p. 102) and the gardens framing the Jacobean House at Hatfield (see p. 46) where she also had the remnants of an earlier Tudor Palace to consider. Although working within this discipline which controls her designs, she avoids rigidity: in both gardens there is a spirit of innovation. New planting themes enforce old styles. Her interpretation of both 16th- and 17th-century styles can be compared with some of the equally scholarly restorations of Natural Trust period gardens. Another example is Hestercombe in Somerset, which was first laid out just before the 1914-18 war; this garden perhaps best expresses the essence of the Lutyens/Jekyll partnership (see pp. 186-7). The gardens surrounding 18th-century colonial Williamsburg in Virginia, restored from 1926 onwards, and the gardens at the Palace of Het Loo in Holland are further examples of successful restorations.

This book describes some of these gardens and others more in keeping with modern architecture and contemporary life styles,

illustrating a wide range of garden themes and ideas. While doing so it demonstrates how infinitely variable are individuals' interpretations of what might seem a quite detailed and exact proposal for a particular garden. Not only are similar ideas handled differently, but decisions on whether to use more or less intensive methods of maintenance will considerably influence the appearance of a 'finished' garden. Gardeners also learn how the site and aspect of a garden will impose a certain degree of discipline, by limiting or extending the range of plants which can successfully be grown. By helping the reader to consider all the relevant factors, an appropriate garden style should evolve.

All garden visiting is part of a process of getting your eye 'educated' to gardening possibilities. Words and pictures can be a useful preliminary to visiting, and become a later reinforcement to gardening awareness. This book is designed to take a reader through a series of steps in an individual's gardening education. Its pictures illustrate a wide range of garden themes and ideas, but it remains to the individual to choose, improve and adapt for his or her own circumstances. Whatever theme is chosen, every gardener will inevitably stamp a very personal style and atmosphere on a garden; this is as it should be. Gardening must remain a personal expression and interpretation.

INSPIRATION
& EDUCATION

Tintinhull . Hidcote . Docwra's . East Lambrook

Hadspen . Abbotsbury . Knightshayes . La Gamberaia . Royaumont

Giardino dei Giusti . *Blake House*

I first became interested in gardening after visiting Tintinhull House in Somerset (it was nearly thirty years later that I came to live and garden there). At that time I was twenty-five and married; I lived in a 17th-century farmhouse where the garden, on a steep hillside, had once been terraced and 'worked' but had been long neglected. One stony border, containing an old mauve-flowered lilac, and a well-tilled kitchen garden of about 1000 sq m (a quarter of an acre) were all that remained of earlier garden attempts. I knew nothing, had no horticultural background and had learned little of wildflowers in my childhood.

It seems fortunate that the gardens at Tintinhull were so carefully designed that even a complete amateur could almost immediately grasp the strong lines of the layout and the colour schemes which defined each garden compartment. The garden was and still is an inspiration. Even then I realised that it is never possible to slavishly copy another garden; what Tintinhull showed me was how design could control garden atmosphere. It also made me realise how much could be learned and absorbed by visiting gardens. Books about gardening and design were stimulating but seeing a garden and feeling its atmosphere was ultimately essential for me and by far my greatest educational guide. Every garden scene, every different plant association, on whatever scale and in whatever conditions of soil or climate, could later serve as a basis for working out one's own garden schemes. Many years later I still believe that most garden consultants draw on garden images, perhaps stored away in the subconscious, which are recalled to fit some new design problem as and when necessary.

At Tintinhull, it was not only the tightness and logistics of the design which appealed to the amateur. Flowers and foliage were so arranged as to convey a series of pictorial images or compositions. Flower and leaf colour and texture were deliberately placed in associated harmonies or contrasts. Effects were illuminating and simple. Gardening was clearly an art closely related to both architecture and painting. The owner, Mrs Phyllis Reiss, who had

planted the garden, was still alive (she died in 1962, a few years after giving the property to the National Trust). She had lived at Tintinhull since 1933; her inspirational colour schemes were already well-known. I had yet to discover how difficult it was to learn enough to attempt similar subtle effects, let alone how to grow plants. Tintinhull is an educational garden, the scale of its parts closely related to the size of many modern gardens. In fact, each of its 'rooms' is self-contained in such a way that any one of them could be a complete single garden.

Phyllis Reiss took her theme from Lawrence Johnston's garden at Hidcote. Lawrence Johnston remains an enigma. Reticent about himself, he combined an architectural view of a garden with the avid plant collector's instinct, yet it is hard to discover his basic garden philosophy; he never wrote about his garden and rarely spoke about it. One of his few recorded comments was made

PREVIOUS PAGES: LEFT Nymans in Sussex, planted and laid out by the Messel family, is a superb example of a garden which combines formal design with a collection of rare trees and shrubs. Features such as topiary are adjacent to the house, leaving 'wild' planting to be discovered beyond the main lawn. A visitor to a garden such as this might well be inspired to adapt elements of its design for use in a much more limited area.

PREVIOUS PAGES: RIGHT Bronze-flowered German irises are planted in a long narrow bed which stretches parallel to the main perimeter wall on the east of the garden at Tintinhull.

LEFT All the paths at Tintinhull are directional aids as well as being functional; walls and hedges enclose volumes of space and mark out vertical lines and barriers. They also provide background colour

and protection for borders. Ascending and descending steps exaggerate changes of level on what is almost a horizontal site; tall evergreen trees frame the skyline. During a garden walk, a visitor constantly moves between areas of shadow and sunlight. All these 'tricks' are used deliberately to make the garden seem larger than it is.

ABOVE The Botanic Garden of Padua University, one of the earliest teaching gardens, was established by Venetian decree in 1545. Its original layout of stone-edged 'order' beds inside a circular wall survives. The garden, primarily envisaged as a means of providing live plant material for students and an apothecary's shop, rapidly expanded to contain a large collection of plants newly introduced to Europe through Venetian contacts.

towards the end of his life during a tour of the garden with American cousins. 'A garden is a metaphysical creation. But is it the metaphysic which creates the garden, or the garden the metaphysic?' We can only seek to understand his meaning by visiting Hidcote and trying to analyse the overall conception, then studying the planting detail. The layout at Hidcote reflects the management of volumes of space which seems essentially derived from the Renaissance garden of the 16th century. Yet, unlike an Italian villa, it seems curiously unconnected with the house. The original windswept site was bare except for two clumps of beechwood and an ancient cedar near the 17th-century farmhouse. The garden was laid out with a pattern of hedges: yew, beech, box, holly and hornbeam, sometimes mixed together to make a tapestry effect. Inside each area formed by these hedge barriers, twenty-one in all, plants were tightly packed in a series of different themes.

This conception of little gardens within a large garden seemed, at that time, original but in fact identifies with the late Victorians' search for an English style. Towards the end of the 19th century, many gardeners had become interested in developing period gardens, often harking back to Tudor or Jacobean formality. Sedding's *Gardencraft, Old and New* and Blomfield's *The Formal Garden in England*, published in the 1890s within a year of each other, both stressed the architectural framework of the garden. The architect should create a strong structure in which the gardener would be allowed to plant, just as an interior decorator would paint and furnish a room in a house. An aerial view of Hidcote would be like a house with its roof off. An enclosed world of regular-shaped rooms lead off each other or are linked by hedge corridors. The visitor to the garden gets no immediate view of surrounding countryside but vistas lead through the series of hedged enclosures to the skyline, which on approach reveals views over the Evesham vale below. Throughout the garden, formality of layout is contrasted with extreme informality in planting.

At Tintinhull, the house is more intimately involved with the garden than at Hidcote. In both gardens an overall unity of design is achieved, not only by paths which link 'rooms', but also by a repetition of the same or similar plants in different areas. At Hidcote yew hedging predominates just as it does at Tintinhull but, in the latter garden, groups of grey-leaved plants such as *Senecio* 'Sunshine' and the bushy, more silvery *Artemisia* 'Powis Castle' are planted in each of the areas. This ensures an absence of restlessness: repetition makes for reassurance and a calm atmosphere.

Mrs Phyllis Reiss lived close to Hidcote during the 1920s. When she discovered Tintinhull in Somerset, she must have realized at once that its smaller area seemed already a miniature version of the larger garden. An old cedar, two mature yew trees and two large *Quercus ilex* provided scale and alternating areas of sunlight and shade. The red border at Hidcote must have inspired her daring

LEFT The white garden below the house terrace at Hidcote is overlooked by the great cedar and framed and decorated with yew shapes, the dark green, almost matt, foliage contrasting with the purity of the white flowers. One-colour gardens benefit from being contained in a firm structure; the garden at Tintinhull has many of the same components.

RIGHT The compartments at Hidcote were classically Italian in conception. Lawrence Johnston's layout has been the prototype for many modern gardens. Here, a vista through one of a pair of gazebos at Hidcote carries the eye along a green alley hedged with hornbeam to a viewpoint over the countryside.

'hot' border facing east in the Tintinhull pool garden and also her purple and gold foliage border which lay close to the canopy of the old cedar. But above all, and more important than its planting detail, Hidcote became a prototype for modern English gardening. The developments at Sissinghurst Castle (p. 194) and later of gardens such as The Courts, Newby Hall (p. 42), Bramdean House and post-war Jenkyn Place (pp. 92-3) are all closely related and strongly derivative. Each has geometric garden compartments, yet each garden is quite different in atmosphere and strongly dominated by the individual owner's personality.

Having seen Tintinhull and felt its atmosphere, I had no desire to copy it. Probably at that time its perfections made it an impossible model. Nevertheless, Tintinhull had opened my eyes to the aesthetic possibilities of gardening. Now it was necessary to learn by taking advice and reading books suitably geared to my ignorance. Fortunately, John Raven, a classics don at Cambridge and later the author of *A Botanist's Garden*, was an old friend. He gave me reading lists and general as well as specific encouragement.

At Docwra's Manor just outside Cambridge, John and Faith Raven made a garden of asymmetric compartments inside a framework of old barns and pigsties which surrounded the Jacobean farmhouse, and created pockets with favourable microclimatic conditions although the soil was alkaline and the rainfall low. More interested in plant species than in 'improved' garden plants, the Ravens developed luxuriant tightly packed planting schemes which, on close inspection, revealed many rare specimens, often grown from seed or bulbs found in the Mediterranean area.

Peonies such as *Paeonia cambessedesii* from the Balearic Islands with red-stemmed stalks like rhubarb, deep pink flowers and decorative foliage, *P. emodi*, *P. mascula* in many of its European forms, and the early-flowering yellow *P. mlokosewitschii* grew next to *Nectaroscordon bulgaricum* with greenish-purple bells opening from strange papery shrouds. The rare *Cardamine enneaphyllos*, closely resembling our native cuckoo flower, came from the meadows near Asolo in northern Italy. To the uninitiated, Docwra's was a cottage garden filled to overflowing with a grand variety of plants; for the expert, it contained many treasures hardly to be seen in other gardens, although John and Faith always made a point of giving at least one specimen of each of their rarities to the Cambridge Botanic Garden. Its style was eclectic, yet the luxuriance of the planting disguised the emphasis on plants of botanical interest. Above all plants were given sites which were likely to please them and where as a result they would spread and seed to give a relaxed atmosphere, part of the garden's charm.

From the Ravens I learned the importance of understanding the conditions plants had in their native habitats and therefore the whole question of plant association which is far from being merely

aesthetic. It is useless to plant alpines from high mountains next to moisture-loving plants from damp meadows; equally hopeless to place grey-leaved Mediterranean-type plants which thrive in poor stony soil next to rich feeders. The education of a gardener ensures that plants which are inappropriate neighbours placed together make as jarring an immediate impression as any garish colour scheme. In the last fifteen years, Beth Chatto's stands at Chelsea and elsewhere have been instrumental in opening many gardeners' eyes and minds to this basic and obvious fact; understanding and accepting it adds another dimension to gardening.

Margery Fish at East Lambrook was a close neighbour in Somerset. Her garden was completely different in style and atmosphere from both Tintinhull House (although she and Mrs Reiss were close friends and shared many gardening experiences) and Docwra's Manor. In her first book, *We Made A Garden*, Mrs Fish describes the simple layout which incorporated an old dry ditch and cider orchard (see also pp. 154-5). By the time I went there at the end of the 1950s, planting was dense, particularly at ground-level, and the quite strong design outlines were obscured. The plants were what mattered. In a small area, hardly more than an acre, there was a collection of rare forms and cultivars of quite ordinary perennials and bulbs. There were countless 'cottage garden' primroses; forty-five different snowdrops; dozens of different hardy herbaceous geraniums; a range of hardy cyclamen, and an extensive number of small- and large-leaved ivies, which she

over are often united by the variety of plants that can be grown within a given site, not by the range of different themes dictated by passing fashions and a wealthy background. To visit this garden became an emotional experience for many; each footstep revealed new and unexpected treasures. Plants were tightly packed together and seedlings were encouraged to flourish. Like Beth Chatto and the Ravens, Margery Fish studied plants and the conditions they required and those they had in their native habitats. She tried, on her basically difficult alkaline soil, to create suitable sites and to give each plant suitable neighbours. By visiting the nursery it was possible to meet Mrs Fish and she became to me, as she was to many others, a patient mentor and teacher.

During this period I was reading Graham Stuart Thomas's books on old and modern shrub roses. These, with low-growing hardy herbaceous perennials such as geraniums, hostas, alchemillas, Solomon's seal, and ajugas massed at their feet, seemed appropriate for the farm garden I had to work in. Species roses such as the prickly white-flowered *Rosa × paulii* and its pink cultivar *R. × p.* 'Rosea' loved to trail downwards over steep terraced walls. Yellow *R. hugonis* and *R. × cantabrigiensis* had ferny leaves and an arching habit. *R. glauca* (in those days *R. rubrifolia*) had grey glaucous leaves, pink flowers and orange berries in autumn. These and shrubs such as the smoke bush, *Cotinus coggygria*, were to be trouble-free, needing pruning at most once a year, and could be underplanted with the dense foliage of plants found at East Lambrook nursery. Following the lead of John and Faith Raven I thought I would, on the whole, limit plants in the garden to species. This idea lasted a short time, as did an earlier notion to limit garden planting to yellow- and white-flowered performers. Visits to East Lambrook meant returning with car-loads of not only the 'type' plant of species, but double or improved strains, and forms with coloured or variegated leaves. It was impossible to visit the nursery without yielding to impulse buying.

Margery Fish made many suggestions and gave me an introduction to a vast new range of genera as well as her rare treasures. Today, long after her death in 1968, she is primarily associated with a cult of cottage-gardening and, in some senses, rural simplicity. She often used popular names for plants in true Robinsonian style, yet she was a stickler for correct botanical nomenclature in her writing and in the naming of plants for sale at her nursery. She also stressed the importance of keeping records of the provenance of unusual forms and varieties.

I was to learn much from Margery Fish on the subject of companion planting: plants and their association and growing them well was her chief interest, much more so than garden design, its history and its development. Visiting her garden became a lesson in observing detail and noticing subtle differences in flower and leaf

mainly used as weed-suppressing groundcovers. Hostas, hellebores, euphorbias and cyclamen of many types combined seasonal flower and foliage interest to carry the garden through all the months of the year. Mrs Fish collected plants with variegated leaves but because these were mainly small in size she could avoid giving the garden a 'spotty' appearance; instead, they came as unexpected surprises growing close to other plants. One of the largest was the variegated form of the Himalayan lilac, *Syringa emodi*, its golden leaves centrally marked with green.

Mrs Fish ran a nursery where many of these plants, some of which could only be increased by division, were available. East Lambrook became a mecca for plantsmen gardeners, its small scale and obvious lack of grandeur and stylistic pretension giving the humblest enthusiast, with perhaps a very small urban or country cottage garden, a sense of security and reality. Gardeners the world

ABOVE LEFT Behind a wall in an outer garden compartment at Docwra's Manor, a group of the green-striped white garden tulip, *Tulipa viridiflora*, with delicate small flowerheads, makes a pocket of light between a drift of euphorbias.

ABOVE In the walled garden at Docwra's, day-lilies, bronze-flowered iris and comfrey are companions to a collection of Umbelliferae. In the foreground sea-kale, *Crambe maritima*, has white flowers; at the back, the elegant fern-like *Selinum tenuifolium*, caught in a shaft of sunlight, has flat white flower umbels.

LEFT Yellow forms of the Scotch rose, *Rosa pimpinellifolia*, flourish in the border on the north side of Tintinhull House. By the 1950s Graham Stuart Thomas's books on growing old roses and their history were available to the public. He encouraged gardeners to grow roses as shrubs in borders, often underplanted with some attractive flowering perennial, rather than only in formal rose beds.

RIGHT ABOVE At East Lambrook a path, defined by clipped *Chamaecyparis*, leads to the pagoda tree, a spreading dogwood, *Cornus controversa* 'Variegata'. A pink-flowered shrub *Kolkwitzia amabalis* underplanted with germander, *Teucrium chamaedrys*, flourishes opposite roses, hardy geraniums and euphorbias. The style, as at Docwra's, is relaxed; emphasis is on plants and their association.

RIGHT BELOW In the silver garden at East Lambrook, Margery Fish used Mediterranean-type plants with aromatic and hairy leaves which prevent water-transpiration in hot climates. The small hairs and leaf texture present a silvery effect; the scented foliage evokes the Mediterranean maquis. Mrs Fish studied the native habitat of her plants and, in her Somerset garden, gave them a situation as similar as possible.

shape and colour. I remember my first planting of the clump-forming *Iris graminea* with its almost hidden, richly-scented purple flowers and the broader-leaved *I. japonica* with its orchid-like blooms, both from East Lambrook. Later she gave me the precious shy-flowering variegated form of the latter. Being new to gardening I failed to realize how rare was her talent, how unusual her plants. It was easy to take for granted that fifteen different polemoniums were available in her nursery, at least nine or ten blue- and red-flowered salvias all with highly aromatic foliage, three or four coloured forms of the Algerian iris, *I. unguicularis*, and even a variegated-leaved bishop's weed, *Aegopodium podagraria* 'Variegata', guaranteed not to become invasive.

In 1968 I moved from the small farm garden to my husband's family home, Hadspen House, close by. The 3.5 hectare (9 acre) garden had been neglected since the outbreak of war in 1939 when much of the garden had been converted to digging for victory. Where previously five gardeners and a boy had worked under a skilled head-gardener, since the end of the war two unskilled labourers had maintained an increasingly small area with brambles, bindweed and ground elder flourishing on the side lines. Shrubs, hidden beneath curtains of white convolvulus, had not been pruned since 1932 and most hardy perennials had disappeared.

The garden at Hadspen had always been divided into two distinct areas. Until the end of the 19th century, parkland surrounded the 18th-century house and a fruit and vegetable garden lay to the north-east. During the early 1900s an Edwardian grandmother, influenced by visits to Italy, took in an area of pasture near the house where she threw out a terrace, added curved stonework and steps and made a circular formal pond. Flowerbeds set in grass on the new terraces were planted with bedding geraniums and other annuals in contemporary Edwardian fashion. The old, more utilitarian garden and rectangular water tank lay behind yew trees to the east and there few changes were made. Both garden areas lay on a south-west facing slope, sheltered and almost encircled by wings of woodland which gave protection from damaging north and east winds. Frost drained freely downwards into the fields beyond the garden boundaries.

After the 1914-18 war there was less labour available at Hadspen but a knowledgeable head-gardener continued the routine planting of annual bedding. The Hobhouses were friendly with the Fox-Strangways who owned the semi-tropical gardens at Abbotsbury on the Dorset coast. Cuttings of rare and somewhat tender evergreens from there were rooted and established at Hadspen. Exotic ornamental trees and interesting shrubs were used in a naturalistic way to enclose the Italianate garden, marking the transition between Victorian bedding and the evolving woodland style of Robinsonian planting.

RIGHT A view from above the old water tank at Hadspen shows the luxuriant growth in this sheltered garden. Many tender climbers and wall plants flourish and seed in gaps in the brickwork. This garden style needs a minimum of maintenance; the most vigorous plants establish a theme and grow together to prevent weed germination.

OPPOSITE LEFT Beneath the high wall and level with the water a new garden bed at Hadspen provides a damp site where rodgersias and other moisture-loving plants are allowed to spread. The strong structural and architectural lines in this part of the garden are a foil to natural plant form, leaf shapes and textures.

OPPOSITE RIGHT The border above the old water tank at Hadspen is backed by a gravel path and a high wall. Frost drains quickly down the slopes at this top end of the garden and terraces provide planting areas where water does not stand in winter.

The slow running down of the garden at Hadspen after the outbreak of war in 1939 was typical of many gardens of similar size and design. Graham Stuart Thomas has said that today one gardener can maintain 4 hectares (10 acres) of garden if the style adopted is not intensive. At Hadspen, during the 1970s and after initial clearance, this proved to be the case.

We had an advantage over earlier labour forces. Modern herbicides could be used to weaken and eventually eradicate persistent perennial or woody weeds. The Flymo, manoeuvrable, under shrubs, had just become available. Many good specimens were found submerged in undergrowth. Some could be saved as perennial weed around them was killed; others had to be dug out and replaced.

The new planting was designed in three layers. Small ornamental trees were to provide overhead canopies for spreading shrubs which in their turn sheltered lower-growing bulbs and perennials. The shapes of trees and shrubs and their leaf colour and texture became the main focus of the garden.

From the beginning we had one full-time gardener to help with heavy work, look after the walled kitchen garden and, as areas of flowerbed were cleared and cleaned, to dig them over and mulch thickly with farmyard manure and any other organic material which was locally available. Gradually the stony alkaline soil began to improve in texture, making it easier to weed and plant. Grass mowing had to be rationalized, so massed evergreen groundcovers

such as *Vinca, Epimedium*, St John's wort and *Symphytum* were planted in island shrub beds where their spreading characteristics could be contained by mowing. This meant that labour-intensive edging was eliminated and yet the garden looked well manicured.

In 1968 I knew little and after the move to Hadspen I had to make use of any experience I had. I had learned some practical gardening by experimenting in the small farm garden. My main interest was in shrubs, their shapes and their foliage and this prejudice in favour of woody plants was to help me in evolving the Hadspen style. Nearly twenty years later it seems simple to stress the design ideas and practical maintenance routine. At the time, clearing and cleaning the garden and gradually establishing a labour-saving style, suitable for the last quarter of the twentieth century, was a painful and exhausting process. Now I feel that the lessons learned were a vital part of my gardening education and I realise that I was fortunate to have the opportunity to work in a practical rather than theoretical way.

Fortunately, my arrival at Hadspen coincided with a new and vigorous head-gardener at Abbotsbury. Besides his restoration of the garden, John Hussey started a small nursery, at first concentrating on the propagation of many of the good plants actually growing in the garden and, in particular, those which were no longer easily located in nurseries. He generously gave me cutting material from those evergreen shrubs which he felt could survive the colder winters of an inland garden.

At the time planting inside the shelter belt was confined mainly to a walled garden, which is still the nucleus of Abbotsbury's much extended set-up. The mature gardens, now covering approximately 7 hectares (17 acres), were first planted in the 18th century and have had a continuous history. Tree and shrub specimens represent the Fox-Strangways family's interest in contemporary plant introductions covering a span of more than a century and a half.

Dense woodland, mainly of evergreen oaks, still provides essential protection from salt-laden winds and creates an almost frost-free microclimate, with high humidity and a rainfall of 68 centimetres (27 inches). The organic soil has a pH of between 4 and 5, allowing ericaceous plants and many South American and Australasian species to flourish. Dogwoods and magnolias from America and Asia have grown huge; mimosas, Chilean myrtle (*Myrtus apiculata*) and griselines, bushes in most gardens, have reached tree proportions. Fine specimens of Chusan palm are 13 metres (40 feet) high and a specimen of *Magnolia campbelli* flowering in March reaches to more than half as high again. There is a fine collection of camellias, many also of tree size, and many large-leaved rhododendrons. On the walls of the original garden area climbers twine in tropical profusion. Rare *Sinofranchetia chinensis*, introduced from China in 1907, *Stauntonia hexaphylla* with heavy scented flowers and a related *Holboellia latifolia*, cestrums from South America and white-flowered solanums grow next to the more ordinary wisterias, akebias and tender rose species.

When I first visited in the early 1960s the gardens were overgrown and neglected. Inside the ring of trees, nature, but not native plants, had taken control. Paths were hard to find and follow. Tropical-style plants with large glossy leaves jostled each other in shade. In open glades Mediterranean-type shrubs with grey and aromatic leaves grew equally luxuriously. In a few years the gardens would have become almost impossible to save but in the short term they had many lessons to offer. I loved the jungle effects and the contrasting leaf textures and shapes. In fact there was little real weed; instead evergreen shrubs such as *Gaultheria shallon* made solid and impenetrable groundcover under taller dogwoods and magnolias. Abbotsbury seemed a forgotten garden paradise, a wilderness rather than a garden. In style and atmosphere, it was in total contrast to the ordered and immaculate Knightshayes Court in Devon which provided the other strand of my education and inspiration at the time.

Obviously, it was impossible at Hadspen to emulate the contrasting styles which were so effective at Abbotsbury and Knightshayes. At the time it seemed essential to establish an overall effect of a controlled wilderness and Abbotsbury taught me about the effective juxtaposition of foliage shapes and textures. It only remained to adapt the actual planting, choosing plants suitable for a colder inland climate. Trees and shrubs, instead of being viewed as perfect specimens as in the woodland garden at Knightshayes, had to support and protect each other. Thus it was essential to plant in dense groups and hope to keep visual effects by frequent and judicious pruning.

In the early 1960s and through Margery Fish, I had been fortunate to meet Sir John and Lady Amory at Knightshayes Court in Devon and their head gardener Michael Hickson. Perhaps no other single garden in England provides more inspiration to the enthusiastic amateur and no owners could have been more generous, in teaching and in gifts of plants, than the Amorys. In fact they did not instruct; rather they shared their knowledge and expertise, always including the aspiring learner in garden talk and exchange.

ABOVE At the water's edge, ligularias and rheums, grown more for foliage effects than for flowers, give a naturalistic effect at Abbotsbury. In the 1960s the garden was overgrown, not with weeds, but with rampant ornamentals which enjoyed the fertile soil and warm conditions. Groves of rustling bamboo stretched beside the stream, giving place to what seemed like acres of gunneras and rodgersias with grooved umbrella-like leaves.

FAR RIGHT An Asiatic rhododendron with large leaves, brown-felted below, makes a focal point at Abbotsbury under the branches of a maidenhair tree *Ginkgo biloba*. Plants with large decorative leaves give a jungle effect and appear to shape the design.

TOP The gardens at Knightshayes include formal terraces and naturalistic woodland; in both areas appropriate planting is particularly well-chosen. The two distinct garden styles are recognizable even to the novice gardener. The view from the main terrace outside the Victorian house carries the eye to parkland and the Devon hills.

ABOVE Planting in each garden area is appropriate to the site. In winter raised glass frames cover the silver-leaved plants in the enclosed terrace garden at Knightshayes and protect them from excessive moisture.

ABOVE RIGHT On the upper terrace pyramids of clipped English yew frame an 18th-century lead cistern which is planted twice yearly with different themes.

OPPOSITE The Knightshayes pool garden is surrounded by yew hedges cut in well-defined shapes to contrast with the rounded heads and soft foliage of ornamental trees.

There can be few better ways of discovering gardening; no academic courses in design or botany could match the range of learning I enjoyed with them.

Knightshayes is one of the most important large gardens to be developed after 1945. There are two distinct garden themes: one, a series of formal enclosures and steep terraced beds close to the house; the other, a 'garden in the wood' (see pp. 146-7). Here, in dappled shade, native and exotic plants are arranged in beds which flow along the contours of the wooded slope. Both areas, examples of restraint and simplicity in planting, have influenced modern designers and have served as examples to the plantsman-gardener, who so frequently indulges in plantomania at the expense of coherent design.

With an acid soil, a free-draining south-facing slope and relatively mild temperatures, conditions at Knightshayes make it possible to grow many tender exotics; this possibility is considerably

enhanced by good gardening techniques which contribute much to the good performance. The tender plants are often given carefully chosen microclimatic conditions and some winter shelter; heavy mulches protect roots vulnerable to low temperatures. Traditional straw and netting 'sandwiches' shield wall plants and are on tripods to form windbreaks for young specimen plants which are especially at risk during their first years. Under the canopies of trees in the woodland, wind-chill factors are less extreme; here plants are carefully sited so that they can take advantage of overhead shelter and yet do not compete for moisture with established roots. Acid-loving woodlanders are planted in raised peat-edged beds in shade; alpines and sun-lovers grow in the terrace border along a walk by the house. At the base of the brick walls of the Victorian mansion, Algerian iris, species tulips, nerines, *Schizostylis* and autumn-flowering sternbergias flourish beside tender wall shrubs and climbers.

Of course, there are many gardens which excel in one or more themes but at Knightshayes all the opportunities of the site have been exploited. I was fortunate to be able to visit Knightshayes once or twice a year just when my eyes were becoming attuned to gardening detail. Notebook in hand, I listened attentively to the Amorys and Michael Hickson; I still continue to visit and learn. The good plants, fine design ideas and meticulous gardening style set a high standard for emulation.

Every garden style implies some sort of reconciliation between a love of plants and the creation of an art form where plants and architecture together make an integrated unit. In recognizing the stylistic relationship between house and garden in a strict historical context, a gardener or garden designer will be better prepared to plan a garden suitable for a particular site. Knowledge and appreciation of garden history become a background 'grammar' to personal gardening ideals.

OPPOSITE At Knightshayes the division between the geometrically designed garden and the woodland is clearly marked, exaggerating the change in atmosphere. The steps from the formal terraces lead into the 'garden in the wood'; there, the planting style is naturalistic although the collector's instinct has never ignored rules of proportion and balance.

LEFT ABOVE In an open glade at Knightshayes the greater celandine, *Chelidonium majus*, with grey-green leaves and pale yellow poppy flowers, is massed with masterwort, *Astrantia major*. Above them Asiatic maples cast light shade. The *Chelidonium* was probably introduced by the Romans. The bright orange juice from its stems has been used for treating warts and eye complaints.

LEFT BELOW In the same glade, a wooden seat under an arching shrub rose makes an inviting resting point. In the wood, all the planting is in dappled shade; roses and many rare shrubs enjoy these conditions and thrive under the protection of overhead branches; great care is taken to plant at a distance from tree roots.

ABOVE The gardens of the Renaissance Villa La Gamberaia outside Florence were restored at the end of the last century. The villa looks out over the water parterre, a 'hall of horizontal mirrors', which fills the oblong terrace thrusting out above vine- yards. Beyond the geometric pools, flanked with regimented bushes of box and yew, clipped arcades in a cypress hedge allow a view into the Arno valley. Paths and plants in ornamental pots divide the stone-edged water sections and centre on a glittering fountain.

FAR RIGHT Boxwood balls in different sizes decorate the central garden; the lines of thick box cut at different heights are typical of an early Renaissance garden.

In the 1970s I had the good fortune to visit many gardens in Italy, particularly those in Tuscany, near Florence, Lucca and Siena. Many of them were of pure Renaissance design, a series of garden rooms linked to a contemporary 15th- or 16th-century villa, the interconnected spaces having a direct relationship with the house itself. All was geometric, in balance and perfectly proportioned. Later ones, Baroque in form, had curving stone balustrades and fantastic imagery and were less inward-looking, with vistas extending beyond the garden perimeter. Nearly all the gardens had been through some period of neglect, some were in decay, others had had modern additions or a form of 'modern' restoration, and a few were completely new creations, simulating a garden of the 16th century or earlier.

Sir George Sitwell's *On the Making of Gardens* (1909) describes the principles which guided the makers of these Italian gardens. His writing and my own visiting introduced me to a new world of garden appreciation. Georgina Masson's *Italian Gardens* became my reference and guidebook. At first, it was just a question of looking at and being in these gardens rather than analysing details of specific periods. The gardens were pure architecture; soaring cypresses in alleys framed the façade of a villa (see p. 71) in strong vertical contrast to groves of grey-green olives in the surrounding landscape. Shade-giving evergreen oaks, *Quercus ilex*, gave shelter and privacy to garden 'rooms' carved out of elegant, if crumbling, stonework terraces. Balustrading and curving walls of nymphaeums hung above reflecting water, or framed cascades where water rippled over steep descending staircases. Lemon trees in giant vases were set in box-edged beds (see p. 70); theatres in clipped cypresses and box provided a stage for statues taken from the *commedia dell'arte* (see p. 76). In many of the gardens there was little flower colour; leaves of cedar, cypress and box in different shades and textures of green provided a soft foil to grey stonework. The strongest contrasts were found in sunlight and shadow, moving and still water, and an atmosphere of enclosed secrecy gave way to carefully planned vistas of distant mountains or river valleys.

By 1974 parts of the garden at Hadspen had been reestablished and I was given the chance to write about my experiences. This book, *The Country Gardener*, took two years to finish. The challenge to complete it forced me into an increased awareness of exact detail and the necessity of analysing garden techniques. Above all it helped me to understand and consolidate what I had learned of botanical nomenclature. In writing about gardening, I realised how essential it was both to know something of the history of garden styles (how the introduction of plants from all corners of the world at various times influenced garden fashion) and to continue visiting and taking notes about many great gardens. I joined the Garden History Society, founded in 1965, and had the opportunity to visit

important historic garden sites at home and abroad, often in the company of scholarly experts who were ready to share their knowledge. In 1976, I visited northern Italy and saw Tuscan geometry in a Veronese landscape in the Giardino dei Giusti.

By the middle of the 1980s, my writing (and in particular *Colour in Your Garden*) had led to invitations to give lectures and occasionally to advise about gardens, at first in Europe and later in the United States. These opportunities for travel have further broadened my experience both of stylistic themes and, most importantly, of gardening possibilities in areas of climatic extremes.

To the English gardener the cold and 'wind-chill' factors tolerated by plants are fairly easily ascertained; on the Continent and in the United States 'zoning' for tolerance of low temperatures becomes complicated by hotter summers which ripen wood, allowing deciduous trees and shrubs to withstand cold better than in English gardens. Plants also have to be considered for their tolerance of heat, and in hot dry climates plants grow only during the winter or rainy season. Garden 'style' must be influenced by these climatic variants.

In the United States many of the best modern gardeners, instead of making gardens of classic European design, make use of native and exotic plants that thrive in the particular site. Others

like Blake House (see pp. 36-7) are based on Italian designs but use exotic zone 10 plants within the traditional geometric layout and allot garden space to more 'natural' areas. I visited this garden in the autumn of 1987 and was struck by the successful adaptation of Italianate principles to the Californian climate.

The gardens at Royaumont are on the outer fringe of the Ile de France. This inland area, far from the Atlantic and the warm Gulf Stream, has a continental climate (zone 7) affected by cold air sweeping across from the land mass of the Siberian plains. Hot, mainly dry summers make irrigation essential. The soil needs rich feeding. In 1985 Baron Nathaniel de Rothschild, with my advice, revised many of the main planting areas; today his English gardener Jim Priest, trained at Kew, continues to replan borders and shrubberies.

The gardens have both formal and informal features. Wide lawns, at first hidden from view by yew hedges, are fringed with woodland providing a background to contoured beds of rhododendrons and camellias and to long borders planted in distinctive colour schemes (see p. 140). The kitchen gardens have been divided into rectangular compartments where flowers are grown mainly for picking (see p. 162). Drifts of perennials and annuals fill the garden with scent and summer flower colour.

LEFT ABOVE From the kitchen garden at Royaumont a line of Italian poplars is dramatic against the sky. In the rose garden pale colours only are used; perennials and annuals are planted informally between rose bushes and groups of silver-foliaged plants. This part of the garden, divided into planting compartments, has a central alley of grass flanked by espalier fruit trees. Trellis-work pillars provide climbing frames for scented honeysuckles.

LEFT BELOW At Royaumont a new border beside the swimming pool, planned to reach its peak in August, is mainly for blue flowers and groups of plants with silvery leaves; white flowers are used for emphasis. Cuttings of the far from hardy salvias and most of the 'silvers' are rooted every autumn and overwintered in frames protected from frost.

RIGHT In the Royaumont main border, backed by a dark yew hedge, the thick planting is of mixed form; shrubs, roses, flowering perennials and lilies are all part of this new composition. The design is held together by six regularly spaced mop-headed *Robinia pseudoacacia* 'Umbraculifera' which introduce a note of formality in contrast to the free planting style.

GIARDINO DEI GIUSTI

The garden of the Giusti in Verona in northern Italy dates from the 16th century or earlier. On a steep hillside above the left bank of the river Adige, the Giusti family, who were originally from Tuscany, constructed a series of terraces where steep steps lead up to a pavilion and viewpoint. Fountains and shell decoration on rocks and an elaborate Renaissance parterre in box once existed, more reminiscent of a Tuscan layout than one usually found in gardens in the north of Italy. Originally each section of the parterre at the Giardino dei Giusti was surrounded by tall cypresses. Today, only box hedges and flowerbeds frame central statues by Muttoni which were installed in the 18th century. The central pathway aligned on the gateway and leading towards the steep cliffs which hang above the garden is still lined with cypresses (but not the original trees) to make a central feature. Broad, shallow steps lead upward but are diverted to left and right below a strange grotesque stone mask set in the cliff above a mysterious grotto.

During the 19th century, the garden was landscaped as a *giardino inglese*, but in this century formality returned, and now a pattern of low box hedges contrasts with the dark soaring cypress shapes as it would have done in earlier times. Thomas Coryate, in his *Crudities* published in 1611, describes the garden as 'a passing delect-able place of solace, beautified with many curious knots, fruits of diverse sorts and two rows of lofty cypresses, three and thirty in rank.' Later, John Evelyn visited the garden and praised the cypresses; a French visitor, Des Brosses, President of Burgundy, got lost in the maze there in 1739 and 'was an hour wandering in the blazing sun'.

LEFT Waist-high trim box hedging, making a pattern of enclosed beds set in gravel walkways, fills the horizontal sections of the garden which lie on either side of the cypress walk. In 16th- and 17th-century Italian gardens, box would have been clipped to less than two feet in height and visitors would be able to 'read' a pattern from the rooms of the adjacent villa; in this case, the design is most clearly seen from the pavilion on top of the cliff. The avenue of cypresses is the main directional axis of the garden; the tall spires link the area below the cliff face with the heights above.

ABOVE Beyond the cypress walk, stone steps between deciduous trees, undercarpeted with evergreen groundcover, lead on upwards to a grotto built in the rock face. Planting on the hanging slopes reflects the informality of the 19th-century layout and is a delightful contrast with the strict uniformity of design in the gardens below.

BLAKE HOUSE

The gardens at Blake House, Kensington, California, now belong to the University of California at Berkeley. In 1922 when the house was built, the site was a wind-swept hillside with picturesque rock outcrops extending to a steep cliff beyond the house to the west; by the 1930s this area had been densely planted with both sun-loving native flora and other Mediterranean-type shrubs, bulbs and perennials which could be grown in the favourable warm climate. Hedges of *Melaleuca* and tall *Cornus capitata* screen the area from a formal rose garden to the south of the house where pines and Californian live oaks, *Quercus agrifolia*, frame a vista to San Francisco and the Golden Gate Bridge across the bay. To the north the ground also drops steeply; here the gorge was planted with groves of native redwoods, *Sequoia sempervirens*, which today provide a shady canopy for tree ferns, native sword fern (*Polystichum munitum*), hollyfern (*Cyrtomium falcatum*), and many woodland plants.

Designed and planted by Mrs Anson Stiles Blake and her sister Mabel Symes (the latter studied landscape architecture at Berkeley), the gardens reflect their interest in native and exotic flora but also their knowledge of Italian Renaissance garden form. To the east of the house, where the main approach leads to the front entrance, the garden design is formal. On either side of the water canal geometric compartments hedged with tender *Syzygium paniculatum*, the brush cherry from Australia with delicate pink young foliage, are thickly planted. To the south, yellow flowers and golden foliage set a theme; to the north, maples shade beds filled with pink-flowered kolkwitzias, *Brugmansia suaveolens*, and spreading clumps of pink Japanese anemones.

ABOVE In the Italian garden at Blake House the central canal stretches towards the wooded slope east of the house entrance. This Californian adaptation is said to be based on the design of the Villa Tusculana at Frascati. Tall trees of *Magnolia grandiflora*, standing as specimens in grass, flank the water. The curving double stair conceals a grotto lined with blue tiles where holly ferns (*Cyrtomium falcatum*) seed in the cool shade.

RIGHT Above the grotto two Irish yews are silhouetted against the wood where tall pink-flowered *Impatiens* and blue-fruited *Dianella tasmanica* thrive in the shade. A pair of sacred bamboo, *Nandina domestica*, frame the entrance to the grotto and purple ipomoeas clamber up over the stonework.

A GARDEN
IN ITS SETTING

The Garden in the Landscape . Relating Garden to House

Aspect & Climate . The Enclosed Garden

Villa Noailles . A Formal Connecticut Garden

A Country Garden in New York . Thomas Church's Garden

A Small Chelsea Garden

Gardens are the result of a collaboration between art and nature. The history of gardening is the history of a reconciliation between man's ingenuity in design, his love of nature, and his pleasure in plants and love of growing them. But for a designer or owner there is a further consideration which influences the style of the garden and the planting. The ideal garden is one which seems to fit into its surroundings without jarring the senses. It is easy to make such a statement but quite difficult to explain and interpret the nuance of meaning behind such a seemingly simple assessment. In choosing a 'style' the individual needs to do more than just make an aesthetic judgment which will be interpreted in detailed plant patterns and plant associations. An appropriate garden design is one that feels right for the house and its surroundings and for the plants; the layout also reflects the owner's lifestyle and needs.

If the house belongs to a definite historical period, then its garden style may best follow the contemporary fashion. Knot gardens and topiary are appropriate to Elizabethan and Jacobean palaces. A formal layout of borders with yew and box-edging provides a setting to later 17th-century houses; this also reflects Edwardian styles when architects, looking back in history, designed a strong garden framework to contain cottage-style planting as dictated by William Robinson and Gertrude Jekyll.

Thomas Church designed gardens in the countryside in California for clients who, in this favoured climate, lived much of their lives out of doors and inevitably round a swimming pool. In their gardens he linked the shapes and lines of a pool with the contours of surrounding hills or riverbeds, but in his own city garden in San Francisco (pp. 62-3) he was more conventional, designing appropriately for an early 19th-century hillside house.

Apart from the special link a garden has with the house it surrounds and frames, it has a relationship with its surroundings in an environmental sense. A site is affected by climate and general aspect which control or at least indicate the type of planting to be adopted. Indigenous trees and shrubs planted inside the garden

PREVIOUS PAGES The gardens of Serre de la Madone, on a steep hillside near Menton, on the French Riviera, were designed on terraces originally constructed for growing olives and vines. Lawrence Johnston, the maker of Hidcote gardens, also lived here, where he was able to experiment with many tender plants. The gardens show his love of a formal framework. As he had done at Hidcote, but in this favourable growing climate, he used plants as architectural features to tie the garden into its setting; cypresses and boxwood, pines and ivy, made a coherent pattern; a lemon house, terrace-supporting walls, stone steps and ornamental pots completed the bones of the layout inside which he planted lavishly.

Today the garden is partly abandoned but many exotics live on amongst crumbling stonework, thriving beside indigenous maquis plants. The main stem of the strange *Dasyliron acrotrichum*, a desert succulent, has collapsed to lie among pelargoniums which survive winter temperatures in this microclimate.

LEFT The Château de Courances, in the forest of Fontainebleau south of Paris, looks out over a formal parterre and water canal into a broad ride cut through the woods. Originally designed by Le Nôtre in the 17th century, the gardens at Courances were restored by Achille Duchêne in the 1930s.

ABOVE At the Palazzo Piccolomini, Pienza, built in the 15th century, the hanging terrace garden was designed to frame the view to the wild countryside beyond the valley. Today raised parterres surrounded in double hedges of box are a work of recent restoration, but are firmly Renaissance in style. The garden, while allowing views to the outer world, remains intensely private.

emphasize regional conditions and act as a link with the locality. At Serre de la Madone (pp. 38-9) and the Villa Noailles (pp. 54-7), the 'style' of the garden layout was based on centuries-old vine and olive terracing dating back to Roman times or earlier; the planting inside the framework is 20th-century, much of it with experimental plants from warm climates comparable to the Mediterranean region. Most Renaissance gardens were made on steep hillsides which were terraced long before they were turned into ornamental gardens; 16th- and 17th-century water cascades and stone stairways simply embellished a purely functional layout.

Gardens can be deliberately sited so that the view of the further landscape becomes an important part of the overall visual impact as at the Palazzo Piccolomini; alternatively, gardens may be designed as hidden oases, remote and secluded from the outside world, where planting and 'style' contrast with any natural vegetation or city planning. This concept is easy to grasp; often even a country garden will be almost entirely 'inward' looking and surrounded by perimeter hedges or woodland, but in one section of it there will be a carefully contrived vista to a distant mountain or valley. A town garden can have a glimpse of a church steeple or some other architectural feature which becomes a focal point to be framed exactly as if it was actually in the garden. Often the background planting to a garden is 'borrowed': the garden plan evolves from and is influenced by the position of trees in neighbouring gardens. The outlook is partly formed by the 'skyscape' framed by tree shapes, and individual branches and canopies which make a pattern against the sky. A garden backed by natural woodland (see A Formal Connecticut Garden p. 58) may be very formal in design to stress man's ideal of order conceived as a deliberate contrast to unplanned nature. Nevertheless the wilder background is an important part of the whole, 'setting off' the manicured enclosures. An extreme example of contrast is the famous topiary garden at Levens in Cumbria (see p. 103) set in a wild romantic landscape.

Most houses, large and small, need some sort of flat platform on which to rest; on slopes this area can be further extended with terraces and connecting steps to adjust levels (as at Newby Hall and St Gauden). In grand gardens the area near the house might be an enclosed unit, the only part of the whole garden that gives privacy and is a place for growing flowers, while the rest of the garden, although definitely man-made and designed, would be intended to appear as part of the landscape. Italian Renaissance, French 17th-century gardens and English Tudor and Jacobean gardens were often divided up into compartments, each for some separate garden theme where plants as well as architecture had some special

Roberto Burle Marx, the Brazilian landscape architect, has created his own distinctive garden style where he places emphasis on the use of native plants. He uses plant groups to build up three-dimensional pictures and to make free-flowing abstract patterns on banks and horizontal ground. This garden in Brazil, designed for Mr and Mrs Montiero, expresses gardening as Burle Marx's ideal of landscape as a perfect blend of art and nature.

RIGHT At Magnolia Plantation just outside Charleston in South Carolina, the woodland gardens, in which rhododendrons, azaleas and camellias flourish, surround natural swamps where native evergreen magnolias (*Magnolia grandiflora*), swamp cypress (*Taxodium distichum*), dogwood (*Cornus florida*) and live oak (*Quercus virginiana*) are reflected in the dark waters. In another area box hedges show 17th-century formality, but it is the enchanted wilderness garden which, hidden and mysterious, blends into this southern landscape.

association and were used in different ways. Often flat areas were laid out in formal patterns to be enjoyed from the windows. This 'compartmental' planning can be readily adapted for a modest-sized garden; if the garden is small it is still possible to have two distinct themes, perhaps formal planting mainly of exotics around a paved terrace, with a more natural style further from the house.

The 18th-century English landscape garden style, where sweeping parkland made an elegant setting for fine Georgian mansions, provided little opportunity for growing flowering plants or for any feeling of intimate seclusion. Owners liked to appear to 'own' the countryside visible beyond the garden boundaries; in the previous century, the French cut avenues through natural forest to give the illusion of the garden literally marching into its depths (see Courances p. 40). As a style this is 'landscape' and hardly counts as 'gardening' but today, with an increasing awareness of environmental values, the idea of a garden gradually and almost imperceptibly fading into a natural landscape is very relevant if the situation permits its exploitation. At Crarae in Scotland (p. 145), introduced species of native trees, genera such as *Sorbus* and birch,

fringe the steep ravine in which the planting is more exotic, and act as a transitional link with heather-covered hills. Patricia Thorpe's garden (pp. 60-1) is designed to drift outwards in this way but the pasture is not 'wild'; small stone walls built by early settlers divide it into fields. The garden now exploits this theme in its changes of level; drainage provides good growing sites for alpine-type plants.

However skilful the gardener, and however well plants are growing, the garden will never be a success if the style chosen for it is inappropriate to the architecture and scale of the house. Cottage-style gardening round a grand mansion looks ridiculous; pleached walks and topiary focused on a modern bungalow are equally unsatisfactory. A house in modern concrete can be surrounded with massed foliage effects, arranged in abstract shapes which flow naturally along the contours of slopes and banks. Roberto Burle Marx, working in Brazil, uses coloured and textured foliage in this way to link modern architecture with desert landscapes but also uses native plants to enrich a background setting of tropical forest (see p. 44).

ABOVE In the sunken garden beside the old Tudor Palace at Hatfield the Marchioness of Salisbury has designed a garden appropriate to the architectural period. An elaborate Tudor knot design, that features only those plants that could have been grown at the time the palace was built, and a box labyrinth are laid out in 16th-century style.

ABOVE Quite different in both atmosphere and scale, the garden at Owl Cottage in the Isle of Wight has cottage-style planting, in which the essence is freedom from historical restrictions and context.

Cottage garden plants were traditionally those easily available; usually from 'slips' and seed rather than from the nursery trade. Roses, poppies and campanulas line a pathway.

ASPECT & CLIMATE

Aspect, for the gardener, includes climate, soil type and texture, extremes of high and low temperature, and also rainfall and humidity. Plant choice for any garden will be limited by all these factors. Nowadays plants are 'zoned'; zoning indicates the lowest temperature that any individual specimen can endure.

Unfortunately, little study has been made of the question of a plant's heat and drought tolerance. A site can mitigate or exaggerate the effects of frost. Most damage is caused when frost lies late in an enclosed area; least damage is done when frost rolls down a slope and escapes out of the garden. South-facing slopes make maximum use of the sun's rays, increasing growing hours in any one season and hastening crop development. The chill factor is also crucial; freezing winds prevent transpiration of leaves and, when combined with low temperatures, will result in dehydration and death. On the other hand, a covering of deep snow protects many perennials through hard winters.

Some ill-effects can be lessened using skilled and thoughtful gardening techniques. In New England, evergreen shrubs and tender wall shrubs are wrapped in netting or plastic to prevent dehydration; in less severe climates even an openwork mesh will give considerable protection. Traditionally, wire-netting 'sandwiches' stuffed with straw were made annually for this purpose and 'wigwams' made with conifer branches were erected over newly planted shrubs.

It is possible to create artificial environments and grow plants successfully in spite of seemingly adverse factors. Soil type and texture can be changed to suit particular plants (see the Dower House p. 192); this is most satisfying when done in formal gardening where plants are given an obviously artificial role; in woodland, where natural effects are sought, it is best

FAR LEFT At Western Hills north of San Francisco it is possible to grow a wide range of exotics from many different natural habitats. *Erithrina crista-galli*, the cockspur coral tree from rainy parts of Brazil, flourishes here; in cold climates it can be grown as a sub-shrub cut to the ground in winter. The division of the western states of America into twenty-four different zones of hardiness is bewildering for the gardener; microclimates abound, created by proximity to the sea, north/south mountain ranges and valleys and variable exposure to wind and sun.

CENTRE LEFT In the middle of the 19th century, inside a heavy board fence which filtered the full force of Atlantic gales, Celia Thaxter made a garden on the island of Appledore off the coast of Maine. She died in 1893, but in 1977 a complete planting resoration was begun using the details in her book *An Island Garden*. Her gardening was experimental in the difficult site; she was a pioneer and her writings reveal her trials as well as her successes. Shown here is the restored garden. Day-lilies, poppies, cornflowers, *Coreopsis* and sweet peas flourish in spite of salt-water spray and extreme summer drought and heat. The garden and its maker were painted many times by the American Impressionist Childe Hassam (1859-1935).

LEFT At Tresco Abbey in the Scilly Isles mild temperatures and high humidity make it possible to grow many exotics from widely different habitats. The gardens are laid out on a south-facing slope, protected from wind by plantings of *Cupressus macrocarpa* and the Monterey pine (*Pinus radiata*). Over dry-stone walling fleshy-leaved aeoniums, blue-flowered *Convolvulus sativus* and pelargoniums have seeded to create an unplanned effect which appears natural.

to grow plants which will thrive in existing conditions. Raised beds and containers give opportunities for making soil mixes for individual plant requirements. Attempts to change soil types in ordinary beds and borders, particularly when trying to make conditions more acid, will only be a short-term expedient as lime soon leaches into the new area from surrounding ground.

In nearly all gardens there are pockets where favourable microclimates exist or can be made to exist, often creating a zone rating well above that scheduled for the region. It is well worth experimenting with plants which belong to a higher zone level. All zoning is useful, but each

garden site is unique. In Celia Thaxter's garden off the coast of Maine or in the gardens of Tresco Abbey (above), protection against salt winds is of prime importance. The best way of deciding if certain plants will do well in your garden is to make a study of conditions in their native habitat and see if it is possible to reproduce a similar environment.

THE ENCLOSED GARDEN

An enclosed garden with no views to the outside world is deliberately conceived as an oasis; today its style can be unique or traditional, patterned and formal or naturalistic and jungle-like. These garden rooms may be considered as extensions of the house and the design need have no link with the surroundings; instead it can be firmly linked to an owner's personality and requirements. The plants can be purely ornamental or functional or both.

The original *hortus conclusus* of the Middle Ages, a small walled or fenced garden sometimes with a shady arbour, reflected a need for seclusion and safety. In Christianity a walled garden became a symbol for the virgin bride and by implication the Virgin Mary: 'A garden enclosed is my sister, my spouse; a spring shut up, a fountain sealed.' Boccaccio, in the *Decamaron*, written in the middle of the 14th century, describes imaginary Italian gardens which mark the transition between the medieval period and the Renaissance. Gardens were walled, fenced or surrounded with impenetrable hedges, yet were essentially places of escape from the troubled world: 'If paradise were constituted on earth, it was inconceivable that it could take any other form.' Although closely related to the Persian water garden (see p. 102) and containing many logistics of the Renaissance garden, these enclosures were hardly likely to survive let alone be recorded as art.

Individualistic design takes these gardens outside the mainstream of gardening fashion; the essence of their spirit lies in their freedom from stylistic pressure. Some are restrained and formal; others are decorated lavishly to give a rich jungle effect. Each represents an individual's private interpretation of paradise.

LEFT In a paved corner of this
secluded courtyard garden,
designed by Mr P. Deroose, shade-
loving plants are carefully arranged
for leaf shapes and textures. Giant
Heracleum flowers above the
ferns, rodgersias and *Agapanthus*.
On overhead wooden beams a vine
makes a cool and shady canopy by
midsummer, losing its leaves and
allowing light through in winter.

LEFT In a narrow town garden in Plymouth, Devon, the walls are densely covered with twining plants, including a pink-flowered clematis, and white lilies grow tall searching for the light. The atmosphere is deliberately crowded, and a mirror behind the railings has been used to increase this effect as well as to reflect more light. This gardening style looks deceptively easy; in reality plants need constant attention to preserve their appearance of health and vigour.

BELOW and RIGHT In a small garden in the centre of New York, ferns, grasses, bamboos and flowering plants arranged in pots create an exotic and luxuriant jungle atmosphere. The house is painted red to complement and enhance the greens of foliage; the waving leaves and textures reflect all essential light filtered by the tall surrounding buildings. This sort of gardening is like flower arranging; pictures are constantly built up and then changed; the overriding aim is to create a green oasis as a contrast to the concrete city desert.

VILLA NOAILLES

The gardens at the villa were planted by Vicomte de Noailles mainly in the years after the 1939-45 war, although he had acquired the house, on a steep south-facing slope, many years earlier. The Vicomte died some time ago but the garden, after a period of comparative neglect, is being restored. The Vicomte chose the site for its abundant water supply which flows down from springs in the hills above. The presence of natural water and the setting in a natural bowl with protection from the north winds, provided a perfect garden aspect.

The layout is simple: terraces, once exclusively planted with olives, stretch westward on the descending slope. On these flat areas, hedged to make private concealed garden rooms, the Vicomte has planted in different themes, using many rare exotics which enjoy the hot summers and comparatively mild winters, as well as Mediterranean plants with aromatic leaves and flowers. Around the house topiary box, cut into strange mounded shapes and niches for seats and statues, frame more intimate 'rooms' for privacy. In the entrance court fountains set in the wall recall the Villa d'Este on a small scale; Curse of Corsica, or creeping baby's tears (*Soleirolia soleirolii*), carpets the stone in soft green.

Tall cypresses and broad-headed trees, sometimes pollarded to provide extra summer coolness, tower above the terraces; forty-year-old magnolias, davidias and poplars are vast, thriving in the hot summers and moisture of the lower meadow. The sound of water is continuous in each garden area; fountains play and gently gushing cascades cross the terraces; a formal stone-edged pool almost fills one of the rectangular gardens.

ABOVE Around a circular pool on the top terrace, pots containing white-flowered hardy arum (*Zantedeschia aethiopica*) are used as features. The garden lies on a south-west slope and yew hedges, clipped into severe shapes, give protection from winds which funnel down the valley.

RIGHT One of the garden compartments, surrounded by yew hedging shaped into curving panels and square clipped piers, is filled with tree peonies, under-carpeted with a lattice-work pattern of pink *Oxalis*. At the end of the peony bed a column, inspired by a fountain from the Villa Aldobrandini at Frascati, has a twisted spiral of tumbling water.

ABOVE and RIGHT A pergola of trained Judas trees, pink- and white-flowered forms of *Cercis siliquastrum* stretches along one of the upper terraces at Villa Noailles. A mass of blossom in spring when flowering before the leaves emerge, this arcade provides a shady green walk in summer.

FAR RIGHT On the terraces below the villa daffodils are naturalized in grass under rare trees and ancient olives.

A FORMAL CONNECTICUT GARDEN

Nancy McCabe lives in northern Connecticut, where her garden, almost carved out of the natural woodland of white pines (*Pinus strobus*) and sugar maples (*Acer saccharum*) which clothes a steep slope behind the stucco house, has been terraced and levelled to give distinct garden areas. Formal geometric shapes with definite planting themes frame the house and contrast abruptly with the wild landscape. In autumn these Connecticut woods are vivid with flame colours of maple and sumach. Nancy McCabe is a garden designer, her own garden with its use of spatial relationships and infilling of luxuriant planting schemes makes a perfect shop window for aspiring clients to ponder and admire. Much of her design work is done for gardens similarly situated in very natural settings where formal and compartmental plans provide strong contrasting themes. Patricia Thorpe's garden in upper New York State (see pp. 60-1) where the garden planting flows into the pastoral landscape illustrates an opposite approach. In the McCabe garden there is no attempt to emulate nature; in fact, the garden layout and plants defy nature's encroachment and bring a strong sense of order.

LEFT The ground close to the south-east side of the house was levelled to make a rectangular lawn; beyond this a metre (3 foot) high retaining wall drops to the next level where, enclosed by simple dark green wooden paling, a central grass area is bordered with perennial flowerbeds. Here peonies, Scotch thistle, *Baptisia*, catmint and sweet rocket (*Hesperis matrionalis*) from the neighbouring woods, all with pastel flower colours, grow in profusion. The beds are edged with old bricks to allow plants freedom to billow and sprawl over the edges.

LEFT In the kitchen garden area old tiles from Savannah line the formal beds between brick walkways. Rembrandt and lily-flowered tulips bloom in spring between bushes of lavender which just survive the cold winters.

FAR LEFT The kitchen garden later in the season shows summer-crop vegetables grown with the flowering lavenders.

A COUNTRY GARDEN IN NEW YORK

Patricia Thorpe, an authority on decorative flower arrangements and author of many gardening books, has made her own garden in Otsego County in upper New York State. Round an old white frame farmhouse, she has created a cottage-style garden where flowerbeds nestle beside low dry-stone walls which, as relics of earlier pioneer farming, have been repaired, or have been built by the Thorpes to provide backdrops and quick-draining sites for alpine-type plants. This network of low terraces, almost disguised by tumbling and scrambling plants, descends to the lowest level where a dump of rusty cars was removed to make space for a pond now ringed with grasses and flag (*Iris pseudacorus*) and Siberian iris.

The climate and terrain are rugged; this area 80 km (50 miles) west of Albany registers Zone 4 for plant material. Few plants are woody; some shrub roses, old favourites such as *Rosa glauca, R. macrantha* and dark maroon 'Tuscany', with an ornamental thorn and a crab apple give height to the central area, while an *allée* of lilac to the north and a hedge of roses to the west provide some necessary shelter without, as would have certainly happened in England, cutting the garden area off from the meadows with which it is fringed. It is a garden set firmly in an old but still untamed landscape. From a practical point of view the success of the garden has depended on Pat Thorpe's thorough knowledge of conditions which individual plants need; it also reflects her interest and enthusiasm for plant rarities. Her skills and knowledge had to be contained within a framework of weekend gardening, the restrictions of which can daunt many makers of beautiful gardens.

By using hardy plants which thrive in the terrain and naturalizing them in drifts and waves of varying heights she has complemented nature's own contours; native and exotic flowers and foliage blend together in perfect harmony.

LEFT and ABOVE Lilies and grasses in a border by the house illustrate Pat Thorpe's garden style. A classic perennial border is made up of groups of plants which thrive in competition and need no staking and little annual maintenance. A close-up shows the grace of poppy seedheads. A new style of American gardening exploits the natural beauty of herbaceous plants, many of which are indigenous and are able to withstand colder winters and hotter summers than are experienced in England. They are chosen for both summer flower colour and attractive seedheads; the leaves, brown or golden after crisp frosts are also decorative.

RIGHT The rock garden area, where well-drained soil and low walls provide a suitable planting area for alpine-type plants, fades away into the pasture beyond the garden boundaries.

THOMAS CHURCH'S GARDEN

ABOVE and BELOW The front garden where box bushes are pruned to give an Oriental effect. At ground level, flowering clivias (*Clivia miniata*) and aspidistras frame a stone figure.

Tom Church's house in Hyde Street, on a steep hill in San Francisco, has two distinct garden areas. In front, from a street lined with olive trees, an entrance shaded with pollarded planes (known as sycamores in California) opens on to a shady yard where tree ferns grow under leafy *Pittosporum*. Ornamental box bushes frame an imposing double stairway at the main door. The steep upward thrust of the steps reflects the spirit of the hillside site. In the inner garden, reached by a central archway under the staircase draped with climbers, the layout and atmosphere is Mediterranean.

Tom Church was born in Boston in 1902 but reared in California. His work as a landscape architect was contemporary with a new style of living and new era of leisure. Perhaps most deeply influenced by a visit to Europe in 1927, he not only compared the climate and gardening possibilities between the Mediterranean area and California but also how gardens are actually used. 'As in Italy and Spain, the pleasure of living out of doors, the need of shade, and the conservation of water are all problems which the Californian gardener must meet and answer.' Outdoor living and a swimming pool were synonymous with garden existence; gardens were of simple design with plenty of functional paving and low-maintenance planting. Usually he separated the garden area from the natural landscape by clipped hedges, but native trees (in California evergreen live oaks, *Quercus agrifolia*, and madrones, *Arbutus menziesii*) shaded and

protected the houses and tied them into their setting. Church's intepretation of garden design changed over the years; in the 1930s he experimented with freer forms, believing that a garden space should have no clear-cut definition; by his death in 1978 he had in many ways readopted a more traditional approach using geometric layouts centred on a house or pool. In his town gardens he placed emphasis on the architectural framework: pathways, steps, fences and trellis, using them with plants to compose a picture with as few distractions as possible. He never wavered from his belief that a garden and house, whether in city or countryside, should suit the life style of the owners and fit into the landscape.

BELOW LEFT and BELOW The enclosed, inner garden where a white wisteria drapes itself over ornamental trellis and a box parterre is set in gravel. Rose bushes are planted in beds between the box and pots are lined up on wooden balustrading.

A SMALL CHELSEA GARDEN

ABOVE A standard yellow-flowered rose dominates a corner where pale primrose petunias and bright-flowered marigolds complete the colour scheme. Each right-angled bed is edged with low-growing shrubs to contain the thick planting. The straight lines of the paving are blurred by the soft foliage shapes of bronze-leaved bugle (*Ajuga neptans* 'Atropurpurea'), thyme, and other low plants growing in between the stones.

In a small garden just off a busy road in Chelsea, Mrs Sainty has designed a garden where shapes of flowerbeds, ornamental pots and trellis work on walls are complemented by plant form. The area is small, no more than 12 m (40 feet) deep and 5.5 m (18 feet) across, yet the various themes and tidy colour schemes cleverly divide the garden into almost separate areas. In a small space designers find that spatial concepts can be carefully handled to create an illusion of extra dimension. Tall plants and large pots are arranged to make pockets of shadow beyond the sunlight and, by so doing, help to make a garden seem larger than it is. Horizontal and continuous paving links garden areas and prevents distraction; garden divisions are not absolute but frames of trellis work and the jutting peninsular flowerbeds confirm a compartmental feeling. Wall, paths and paving give architectural coherence. Inside this framework plants, the living organisms, spread and soften the harsh outlines of masonry. Mrs Sainty moved here from a much larger country garden and has used plants and containers in the smaller space without concession to the reduction in scale.

OPPOSITE, RIGHT The trellis work arcade frames a view into the garden where a large container overflowing with flowers and leaves occupies the centre stage. Balls of clipped box grown in handsome black urns emphasize the framed picture. In a small garden, where horizontal planting space is limited, plants grown as standards and decorative pots increase the potential.

ABOVE Looking back towards the trellised sitting area the massed ageratums give coherence and contrast with the yellow and white flowers in the copper pot. The standard roses give the illusion of a hedge, separating the garden areas.

GARDEN
STRUCTURE

Designing a Framework . Avenues . Hedges . Evergreen Framing
Archways & Pergolas . Paths & Steps . Water Features
Jenkyn Place . A Russell Page Garden . Great Dixter

The previous chapter discussed the advantages and limitations of the site and its surroundings, illustrating gardens which either merged with their settings or which were in deliberate contrast to a landscape or an urban complex. This chapter moves on to the basic garden layout and examines the structural components – paths and areas of paving, lawns, trees, hedging, pergolas and other features – and how they can contribute to the overall style of the garden. These form the garden's architectural framework and give it its unity: a combination of hard building materials and living plants inside which more ephemeral and colourful 'secondary' planting schemes are contained. Without this framework the secondary planting, however pretty, may lack coherence and fail to satisfy.

Interestingly, in many successful gardens, when the secondary planting has matured, the garden framework may become unobtrusive and quite difficult to analyze, but its very existence gives an air of purpose. It also provides strong and dense shapes, whether of walls, fencing or evergreen shrubs and hedges, which are essential backdrops for brighter flower and leaf colours.

A black and white photograph of a garden, or a pencil sketch using just vertical and horizontal lines, will reveal the garden's components without the distraction of colour – just as the winter picture of the Canneman garden (pp 66-7) clearly gives its shape and outline. In monochrome, plants become structural and have density and weight, contributing balance and rhythm. They are playing architectural roles, whether singly as focal points, in pairs or groups to frame a scene, or arranged in a continuous line as hedges or, like grass or other groundcover, massed together in a horizontal carpet. Plants form the bones of the garden through all the seasons.

The structure of a garden does not have to be complicated; in fact, as with all garden themes, an essential element is simplicity to achieve balance. It is the fussy, over-elaborate design which can damage the garden's atmosphere, especially where space is restricted. To avoid a feeling of restlessness, smaller gardens should have fewer features; a simple planting scheme used in a part of a large garden is often suitable for adapting as a complete theme in a small one. Because the owner or designer of a large garden has plenty of space to organize, he or she seldom makes the mistake of overcrowding features or including too many themes within a single view. In a small garden the reverse is often true. I believe that it is essential to visit large well-designed gardens in order to train the eye to a sense of proportion and balance.

The brilliant small garden is a synthesis of great ideas, adapted to a limited space. Unity and purpose can be quite simply achieved. For example, a well-placed tree or two to balance with the mass of the house and to frame the sky, supported on the horizontal by smooth lawn together with any necessary functional and directional paths, will be quite sufficient.

In most gardens there will already be man-made features which contribute to setting the scene, the hard materials which complement softer textured plant foliage. In some modern gardens, walls, steps and paved areas will dominate and planting will be rather like

LEFT A formal layout of low hedges, where corners are given accents with clipped domes, is suitable for a flat area and can easily be adapted to suit different scales. Here at Seven Pines in Pennsylvania, dark foliage provides a perfect foil for statuary within a simple grass setting. Formal gardens need not be elaborate. Evergreen hedges and clipped shapes make interesting outlines without distracting flower colour.

ABOVE Arcades cut through tall hornbeam hedging accentuate the architectural quality of this garden, La Mormaire, near Paris. Apart from the pool, the architecture is all living: the hornbeam and yew hedges, the yew pillars in square bases and other topiary shapes, low box hedging and an Italian poplar give marvellous contrasts of texture and scale and frame the lawns, flowerbeds and water. Hedging gives protection from wind and establishes the garden framework, which is complemented by simple 'furnishing': colour and plant themes are kept in separate areas, and planting is in broad masses.

RIGHT Lemon trees in pots and trim box hedges line a path leading to a stone niche, a device which easily adapts to much smaller situations. The early 16th-century Villa Vicobello, near Siena, and its terraces, which descend steeply below the walled lemon garden, were designed by Baldassare Peruzzi (1481–1537) for the Chigi banking family. The garden is typical of its period: a series of 'rooms' on different levels are arranged round the villa, and axial pathways are centred on gateways and doorways.

OPPOSITE LEFT Long slender afternoon shadows make a strong diagonal pattern along the ground between the soaring cypresses that form this striking avenue. The baroque-style Villa Cetinale, near Siena, was built in 1680 for Cardinal Flavio Chigi, a member of the same banking family. The architect was Carlo Fontana (1634–1714), a pupil and collaborator of Bernini. From an imposing double flight of steps on

the north façade, the view looks up the avenue to a hermitage set in deep woodland on the hillside (built by Cardinal Chigi in penitence for crimes committed in his libertine youth).

OPPOSITE RIGHT At Cranborne Manor in Dorset, pollarded limes are severe when leafless in winter but more graceful and cool in summer. Originally a device for creating shade, pollarding, by

lopping back all growth to the trunk, induces the formation of spreading branches and large leaves just above head level. This practice is more familiar in Europe where summers are generally hotter.

furnishing a room, where wall and floor colours cannot be changed. Of the many different materials available for garden-making, some are in harsh and unattractive simulated stone, sharp-edged modern brick or concrete, which, having little texture, associate poorly with plants. Equally, there are many of superb quality and it is worth searching for the best. Materials used should be as sympathetic to the architecture of the house as possible; if the house is of brick or stone, use the same for garden buildings.

As structural components, walls and hedges are interchangeable, while garden features such as arbours, pergolas and trellis work become frames for climbing plants. Trellis is particularly useful as a means of creating separate areas within a small garden. It takes up much less space than a hedge and provides two vertical surfaces on which to grow plants, or it can give a facelift to ugly walls. Paths often look best when built in the same material as the paved terraces which surround the house, and, by continuity, act as links between separate garden areas uniting the whole design.

Grass walks extending from or joining areas of lawn have the same quiet and restful effects.

By pleaching a row of suitable trees, such as hornbeam, lime or chestnut, a narrow, 'raised' hedge is formed. The espalier system of training, traditionally used for fruit trees, makes a decorative openwork pattern along the edge of garden paths. A true plant tunnel has no wood, brick or metal supports, but a similar effect can be achieved by planting two rows of trees not more than 3 metres (10 feet) apart and training their branches on metal hoops to make an arched, covered walkway.

All these features, used sympathetically and in relation to garden scale, are tools in creating layouts of more or less intricacy. Generally speaking, the hard materials will cost more in the first place but will be less demanding for day-to-day maintenance than plants, which not only need suitable growing conditions and skilled care, but also demand precise training, cutting and feeding to fulfil their architectural role.

AVENUES

Avenues of single tree or shrub specimens, where planting is spaced out but
symmetrical, are decorative forms that
give the illusion of a physical barrier.
Espaliered or pleached trees form an
unbroken line, and take up less ground
space than continuous hedging. This is
particularly useful in smaller gardens, and
also allows for companion planting
beneath the linear branches.

Although avenues are generally formed
by successive pairs of trees flanking a
drive, walk or pathway, often by linear
perspective giving an impression of
distance, in fact any pair of objects can
perform a similar function. Ornamental
pots, statues, or a double row of stakes
give the same direction to the eye as lines
of trees, domes of clipped box or yews.

Avenues, by definition, consist of pairs
of identical shapes. To ensure that each
member of a pair is of uniform
appearance and growth, identical plants,
rather than variable seedlings, should be
used and vegetatively produced. Even a
slight variation in aspect can lead to the
plants growing at different rates and
distorting the essential symmetry.

RIGHT ABOVE At Barnsley House in Gloucestershire, an avenue of lime trees is pleached to form strongly architectural aerial blocks of tight foliage about 2 metres (5 to 6 feet) above ground level. Trunks are kept bare to the required height and side branches, at first kept rigid on tight wires, are trained horizontally. At the base of the lime trees small bulbs grow through the glaucous foliage of Jackman's rue. The lime walk leads into the well-known laburnum tunnel which is centred on a sundial at the furthest side of the garden.

RIGHT BELOW Old espalier apple trees, no longer needing supports, make a low, informal avenue stretching away from the north side of the house at Cranborne Manor. Beneath their trunks, scented *Dianthus* 'Mrs Simpkins' forms a simple pattern of white flowers and silvery foliage.

There are many advantages to spaced planting rather than root-hungry, continuous lines of hedging. Training fruit-trees and bushes into ornamental shapes, besides being practical, makes a link between flower and kitchen garden, stressing dual roles of beauty and usefulness.

FAR RIGHT At Hatfield House in Hertfordshire, double rows of standard evergreen oak, *Quercus ilex*, edge gravel paths overlooking the planting on the east terrace lawn. Specially imported from Italy where they take as much as ten years to grow and train, the oaks, which are annually clipped into shape, are not reliably hardy. However, their density of growth makes them most effective grown as symmetrical mop-heads with corresponding clearly defined shadows, planted either in a row or, as here, in avenues.

HEDGES

A tightly clipped evergreen hedge makes an excellent foil for colourful planting schemes as well as providing shelter; lighter-textured hedges provide pleasing effects of filtered light and still form an effective barrier. Low, trimmed hedging, such as *Santolina* or lavender, sets off formal as well as informal planting schemes, and less compact forms, such as catmint, soften hard-edged paved or gravel paths.

Species that respond well to clipping are evergreens such as yew (*Taxus baccata*), box (*Buxus sempervirens*) and holly (*Ilex aquifolium*), and deciduous hornbeam (*Carpinus betulus*) and beech (*Fagus sylvatica*). Quickthorn (*Crataegus monogyna*) and field maple (*Acer campestre*) are particularly suitable for a dense perimeter barrier, while evergreen cotoneasters, escallonias and the winter-flowering *Viburnum tinus* create a freer, more informal style of hedging. Roses (especially rugosas and the late-flowering American suckering *Rosa virginiana*) form dense yet prickly barriers throughout the year. In warm climates, shrubs such as bay, griselinias, olearias and Chilean myrtle (*Myrtus apiculata*) can be used.

If the hedge is an essential part of the garden structure, it must be chosen for lasting qualities. For this reason, I would discard many of the feathery textured conifers, such as *Thuya*, certain types of *Chamaecyparis* and, above all, × *Cupresso-cyparis leylandii*, which, as they grow, become bare and woody at the base. *Lonicera nitida* requires clipping three or four times a year and tends to sucker, growing steadily in width. It is also easily damaged by heavy snowfalls and is not to be recommended for hardy hedging.

LEFT Hedges can be trimmed and trained in ornamental shapes to complement an architectural design or to break a horizontal line. In this garden in Hanover, Germany, high hedges of clipped hornbeam line a gravel path, creating a cool, shady alley. At a central point, the hornbeam has been trained over metal supports to allow for paths to cross and to provide a frame for the stone urn viewed in the distance.

BELOW A continuous row of planting at any level gives structure to a garden, whatever its scale. Here, in a garden by Mrs van Roosmalen in Rekem, Belgium, a lavender hedge, backed by regularly placed domes of feathery false cypress, makes a feature of a patterned stone pathway, both softening its edges and distinguishing it from the adjoining horizontal surfaces.

RIGHT ABOVE At the Villa la Pietra just outside Florence, yew hedges clipped into formal shapes frame the stage of the green theatre and provide a dark background for elegant Venetian statues. Small box domes represent the footlights. The structured gardens at La Pietra are Renaissance in spirit and were created in the first years of this century by Arthur Acton, father of the writer Sir Harold Acton, to frame the villa which dates from the late 15th century. Broad terraces on descending levels are linked by steps and paths which, with tall hedges of cypress, yew and box, divide the whole area into a series of secret rooms. Dark and refreshingly cool in summer heat, the rooms have little floral embellishment, relying for effect on the contrasts of textured foliage and the fine statuary.

RIGHT BELOW At Parnham in Dorset, the furniture-maker John Makepeace and his wife, Jennie, inherited a garden which was laid out in Edwardian grandeur during the early years of this century to complement the Elizabethan house. On the lower terrace, the lines of parallel water channels are accentuated by an avenue of dome-shaped English yews. To either side on the wide lawn, more yews, to make a total of fifty in all, give a sense of scale to achieve architectural balance with the mass of the house. The Makepeaces are replacing some of the yews lost in the intervening years.

FAR RIGHT In the formal gardens at Filoli in California, low curving walls festooned with the creeping fig, *Ficus pumila*, surround a sunken inner garden overhung with spring-flowering trees. The density of the cylindrically shaped Irish yews contrasts with the delicacy of the blossom.

ARCHWAYS & PERGOLAS

As a device to frame a view or as a focal point at the end of a vista or seen across a lawn, an arch, arbour or pergola (or indeed any garden folly or other device) becomes an important part of the main garden structure. A pergola is simply a series of arches; its structure can be decorative in its own right or, clothed with climbing and twining plants, it can lose its separate identity. It has stronger impact as it functions as a pathway, drawing out perspective in a small area and inviting a visitor to walk along its length. As effectively as any hedging screen, it can close in a view, masking unwanted surroundings or, in a larger garden, separating areas.

FAR LEFT In Charleston, South Carolina, Mrs Roger Hanahan's garden is divided into two distinct planting areas. In the foreground, well-laid-out formal brick-edged beds are in full sun; the shady tree-lined garden at the back is reached through a white pergola clad with a yellow banksian rose (known in South Carolina as Lady Banksia Rose). The planting in shade is lush and green, designed to be refreshingly cool in the very hot summers. Many of the plants are traditional ones that would have been found in Charleston gardens during the 18th and 19th centuries.

LEFT A pointed metal arch frames an entrance to an inner garden where the shape of the box-edged bed echoes the ogee point of the archway. Symmetrically-placed box domes, a central standard rose and even the irises with their spiked leaves, are all carefully planned to enhance the composition in this garden designed by Mrs van Roosmalen in Rekem, Belgium.

ABOVE Terracing on steep slopes, originally for vines and olive groves, provides the modern owner with a ready-made garden layout. South-facing level terraces, connected by steps, become a framework for decorative yet practical features. Here, at La Chèvre d'Or, lemon trees are trained on a simple wooden pergola which runs along the high terrace wall, taking advantage of the sun for ripening fruit and making a cool, shady walk.

ABOVE An unusual winding stone pergola at Newby Hall near Ripon, North Yorkshire, was designed by Miss Ellen Willmott in the early 1900s. Originally, the pergola was for a collection of gold and silver variegated ivies with interesting leaf shapes. Today it is resplendent with hanging tassels of laburnum. Wide drifts of glossy evergreen bergenias spill over the local York flagstones, giving winter interest.

ABOVE A narrow fruit pergola, constructed with simple wooden laths bent to make arches, is 17th-century in inspiration, and is reminiscent of the ornamental treillage in vogue then. Some versions of it were used as screens to link buildings with the garden (see p. 64). Here, at New Place, Oxfordshire, the long trellis tunnel with its tall sides and narrow walking space is intended to convey a sense of distance.

ABOVE At The Grove in rural Oxfordshire, a narrow rustic pergola stretches for nearly a hundred metres (over 300 feet). Planted only with the rambling rose 'American Pillar' which bears wide clustered flowers of vivid pink, it is a magnificent sight in early July. For the rest of the year the pergola, designed by the owner, Mr David Hicks, provides a decorative feature to complement the garden's many hedges and pleached trees.

PATHS & STEPS

A functional pathway follows the shortest practical route between two places, hence the cottage garden straight path from gate to door. Straight lines are more economical of space than those which curve, but a meandering path disappearing invitingly round a corner adds an air of mystery to a garden, replacing geometry with carefree informality. A mown path through rough grass implies purpose as well as being decorative, the lawn contrasting with the long textured grasses.

In formal gardens, decorative paths in paving, brick or gravel are arranged as important axial lines as well as defining the edges of beds or separate planting themes. Paths may lead to focal points, be centred on doors or windows, stop and change direction at corners, divide garden areas and, often edged with hedging plants, are used to emphasize linear perspective to increase or diminish distance. A path which narrows as it proceeds is a device for making it appear longer.

Pathways lined with high, enclosing hedges, or more tunnel-like, with two rows of trees trained to form a covered walk are the English 'alley', the French version of which, *allée*, is a walk cut through forest.

Steps to link levels are necessary if a slope has an angle of more than 25 degrees. Greater than that, walking is uncomfortable, and at 45 degrees mowing becomes difficult (although air-cushion mowing machines can cope with steeper gradients). Steps in stone or brick or, more rustically, in grass or gravel edged with lengths of timber, can be decorative features.

RIGHT In 1951 Thomas Church designed a town garden in San Francisco with views over the bay. The design was for Jean Wolff, who was herself a knowledgeable horticulturist and chose the plants to furnish it. Church believed that in a 'good' composition details were to be subordinated to a dominant theme. His firm outlines and architectural structure made a setting for her interesting plants. Steps, retaining walls and clipped hedges on three different levels make a diagonal garden axis, reinforced by a central dividing box hedge in the middle garden which completes the sense of order and purpose. Here, the steps are of contrasting dark timber which gives them emphasis.

LEFT Four shallow steps with long spacious brick treads outlined with timber wind gently up a slope in this garden in Wemeldinge, Holland, to give a feeling of ease and connect two garden areas without an abrupt transition. Thick planting screens the banks at either side and a pair of ornamental pots placed on the outer edge of the second step frame the pathway and invite a spectator to move on and upwards. Paths and steps are essentially lines of communication; building them on a generous scale with wide treads and low risers, avoids an impression of restriction.

LEFT Diamond-shaped stone flags set in mown grass give a strong and purposeful direction without distracting the eye and spoiling the sense of space given by the lawn. Set below the grass level, the stones make maintenance simple, and also keep the feet dry.

RIGHT At The Gables in Somerset, a paved path, part of a formal design for an enclosed garden, is aligned on a central sundial. The sharp edges of the path are disguised by a riot of plants which spill over the sides. A hard surface is a good foil to soft plant shapes and billowing foliage.

WATER FEATURES

Formal water features make no pretence of appearing to imitate nature. Tanks, pools and canals hold still, reflecting water; fountains and cascades cool the air and fill it with movement and sound. A simple formal pool in a modest modern garden adds a dimension to a garden layout, providing not only reflections of sky, trees and buildings, but another planting medium where waterlilies or tall iris spikes make a pattern of surface or vertical shapes and sculptural leaves. While good water features are so desirable in a garden, unfortunately modern fountains and ready-made pool shapes are often inappropriate.

In California, Thomas Church designed pools for private gardens using patterns based on the fluidity of water-forms such as those found in a fanning-out river estuary. At Sutton Place in Surrey, the Paradise Garden designed by Sir Geoffrey Jellicoe is reached only after passing over hazardous stepping stones set across a moat; swirling paths lead to fountains protected by rose-covered arbours. Perhaps inspired by Japanese gardens in which water features were often shaped to resemble animals, Sir Geoffrey has designed a lake in the shape of a fish to symbolize the birth of civilization. Two large mounds and one small one formed from the spoil represent man, woman and child.

Today's designers, often working in gardens for public enjoyment, reinterpret the symbolism of water using great spectacles such as rushing rivers and falls. In Portland, Oregon, Lawrence Halprin designed the Lovejoy Plaza (1961) in abstract rock forms to involve the individual passer-by, combining excitement with just a hint of danger.

LEFT At Brockenhurst Park in the New Forest, Hampshire, a wide canal constructed in the 1870s is Italian in conception. It stretches away from the house to end at a raised terrace reached by a double stairway. On either side of the still water, its stone edging softened by overlapping bushes of herringbone cotoneaster (*Cotoneaster horizontalis*), are green and golden topiary forms. Behind the topiary, double hedges of clipped bay make a sharp frame, above which tall conifers and Luccombe oaks outline the sky. The whole scene is intentionally theatrical, the clipped evergreens providing a perspective where exits and entrances evoke real drama.

ABOVE Broad, shallow stone steps set in mown grass and flanked by shrubs and trees descend to a pool of water at Cornwell Manor in Oxfordshire. Paving and steps should always be generous in scale, unifying garden areas rather than emphasizing divisions. The soft, billowing willows framing the round pond, with its smooth surface and gentle reflections, lend a timeless tranquility.

ABOVE In a modern town garden in Bruges, designed by André van Wassenhove, a rectangular tank with low brick walls becomes the focal point inside a formal layout of clipped hedging. In contrast, other planting is soft and luxuriant with the leaves of royal ferns (*Osmunda regalis*), rheums and rodgersias, and flag irises (*Iris pseudacorus*) giving vertical accents.

RIGHT At Alderley Grange in Gloucestershire, naturalistic planting spilling over the low pond edges deliberately disguises the shape and construction of the pond. The association of architectural form of both plants and hard materials is the basis of good garden structure. Grasses with variegated leaves and arching lady's mantle (*Alchemilla mollis*) grow by the edge; water lilies make rafts on the surface leaving little clear space for reflection.

LEFT At Tintinhull, a central canal separates grass panels and flower borders. Water lilies are carefully spaced out to leave room for reflection of trees and sky. Irises, the common flag and the Japanese *Iris ensata* (syn. *I. kaempferi*), have become corner features leaving the main surface free for swooping swallows.

BELOW In a small city garden, a rectangular formal pool has informal planting round its sides, with drifts of plants at the water's edge having their shapes repeated at the higher level of the pond surround. The jungle effect is deliberately contrived, and the water treated as an extra bed in which to plant. The garden has a sense of space and freedom, but at the same time leafy screens of tall grasses and bamboos give an air of secrecy and remoteness from the world outside.

JENKYN PLACE

LEFT Stretching south from the house a vista between tall trees reveals the distant countryside; a manicured lawn, curving out of sight, invites exploration. In any large garden, mature trees fill three-dimensional space and, by framing the skyline, are as important to the overall garden atmosphere as features at eye or ground level. Trees, by casting shadow and sending out roots to take essential moisture, tend to dominate design decisions and influence all planting patterns.

RIGHT The central axis of the garden around which all the other 'rooms' are organized. Low hedges of yew protrude as buttresses to separate flowerbeds planted in different themes, where stone steps adjust levels on the sloping ground. The long narrow vista crosses the hidden herbaceous border garden and is terminated by a lime tree, under which is an old well.

ABOVE An arch in an old wall allows a glimpse into the Dutch garden, originally part of farm buildings, where flowers and foliage soften the stonework. The climbing rose 'Madame Plantier' and a golden-leaved bay, *Laurus nobilis* 'Aurea', flank the entrance.

At Jenkyn Place in Hampshire, the garden is elaborate, with ornamental features and many hidden compartments. It is a formal garden where design possibilities have been fully exploited, and it is also a fine plantsman's garden where rare trees and shrubs are grown successfully on the hospitable greensand. An enclosure near the elegant William and Mary house contains a vast cedar of Lebanon, planted in 1823. Established ilex, limes and a tulip tree frame distant views of a chalk escarpment beyond the Wey valley. The garden areas lie on a gradual slope mainly to the south and west. Mr and Mrs G. Coke, who came in 1941, levelled the areas, connecting them with steps and aligning main vistas through each separate 'room'. Views narrow and widen to give a feeling of space and distance which acts as an inducement to further exploration.

Each garden area is planted differently: themes include a rose garden; a hidden garden, its walls curtained with rare climbers; magnificent double herbaceous borders facing each other across a panel of lawn; gardens for separate genera such as lupins, peonies and crinums; a circular herb garden hemmed in by espalier-trained apples; and a broad alley lined by tapestry hedges in green and copper beech. With growing appreciation one senses the choice and precision of mature plantsmanship. Rare trees and shrubs such as a flowering Chinese yellow-wood (*Cladastris sinensis*), evergreen *Arbutus × andrachnoides* and *Viburnum cylindricum* catch the eye, while the tall tulip trees, evergreen oaks, chestnuts and limes give an ageless maturity to the garden scene. Jenkyn Place achieves a happy blend of formality and freer planting style.

A RUSSELL PAGE GARDEN

Russell Page's design for a suburban garden in Kortrijk, Belgium, is a fine example of the use of unifying structure which holds a scheme together while allowing the furnishing plants to perform an architectural role.

Like many garden designers, Russell Page (1906-85) studied painting before beginning his career in landscape design. Many of his most important gardens were in Europe and America, although he himself was English. He says in *The Education of a Gardener* (published 1962) that his own development of style was more dependent on the clear cut formality of French gardening than on the eclectic English tradition. In France plants

conformed to design; in England plants tended to take over and discipline was often lacking in favour of developing the plant's natural form. Russell Page not only had a strong sense of structure but also had a knowledge of plants so that he was able to use them as the living tools of his trade.

Started in the 1960s, some areas of the garden in Kortrijk were finished by the Belgian landscape gardener Jacques Wirtz. In the white garden, Russell Page's pathways in soft brick form irregular patterns between Wirtz's geometrically arranged box-edged beds planted with strong-growing herbaceous perennials (see pp. 116-7).

BELOW A row of pleached limes allows a glimpse of the white garden, with its planting scheme added by Jacques Wirtz: box-edged flowerbeds containing strong foliage forms are seen over a group of flowering lady's mantle, *Alchemilla mollis*.

RIGHT In the borders shrub roses, campanulas and strong-growing perennials cover the earth in rich profusion. This sort of gardening works well when linear forms dominate the planting schemes; without the strength of both vertical and horizontal accents, the garden would appear quite commonplace.

BELOW LEFT Irish yews and clipped pillars of English yew, a reminder of Lawrence Johnston's garden at Hidcote, flank paths and mark corners in this Belgian garden. They also divide it into sections. These plants are arranged in a formal rhythm, dictating a uniform pattern and theme inside which gravel and mellow brick pathways, set at right angles, contribute a horizontal ground plan between the smooth lawns.

GREAT DIXTER

Great Dixter lies 16 kilometres (10 miles) inland in East Sussex, close to the Kent border. The gardens were laid out by Edwin Lutyens for Mr and Mrs Nathaniel Lloyd in 1911; he also restored and added to the 15th-century half-timbered house which is at the centre of the 1.5-hectare (6-acre) garden. Lutyens divided up the garden into a series of asymmetrical compartments, incorporating old farm buildings and cattle yards as part of the layout. Background walls are of different heights and meet at odd angles so that paths and vistas sometimes seem deliberately confusing and appear most logical when related to the house itself. South-facing, sitting on a slope which allows free frost-drainage, the house is 250 metres (over 800 feet) above sea-level; the garden aspect would be cold and exposed without the sheltered 'rooms' and the mature wind-filtering hedges. The soil (basically neutral Wadhurst clay) has been worked for many years and manure and compost have improved the texture.

Nathaniel Lloyd was an architect and an authority on topiary and he himself designed the sunken garden and octagonal pool which were added in 1923. Yew topiary specimens of birds and abstract shapes, and hedges clipped as castellated battlements reflect his interests. Mrs Lloyd was a gardener and plantswoman; her influence is seen in the extensive areas of meadow where native and exotic flora are naturalized in the rough grass. Early crocus are succeeded by snakeshead fritillaries (*Fritillaria meleagris*), summer snowflake (*Leucojum aestivum*), purple *Orchis mascula* and oxeye daisies (*Chrysanthemum leucanthemum*). By July the spotted orchis (now *Dactylorhiza fuchsii*) are in flower and mowing is put off until seed is set.

The Lutyens plan provided a layout where two generations of Lloyds have gardened. Christopher Lloyd's style is that of a plantsman who uses daring and experimental colour schemes inside an existing and disciplined framework; his father's decorative topiary remains an important feature, his mother's pioneer meadow-gardening has been expanded beyond the approach orchard and the dry moat. Everywhere, even in the formal rose garden sited in the original cattle yards, planting is mixed, with seedlings of good plants encouraged to thrive in haphazard fashion. His own writing has influenced new generations of gardeners, who have been encouraged to discover a free style of planting rather than being constrained by allotting separate garden areas to definite plant types. Seedlings of *Verbena bonariensis* and bronze-leaved *Oxalis acetosella* (a weed to many) grow in his rose beds; *Clematis* (the small-flowered species) clamber on poles between the rose bushes. In the orchards, old apple trees have become hosts to vigorous cluster-flowered roses which perform in July above the luxuriant meadow grass and wildflowers.

FAR LEFT The mixed border at Dixter is the most photographed border in Britain. Edged by wide flagstones, it stretches east from the terrace below the house 60 metres (200 feet) long and 4.5 metres (15 feet) deep. In it small trees, shrubs, shrub roses, perennials, biennials, annuals and bulbs jostle in broad sweeps of colour. Christopher Lloyd is skilled in the management of this complex garden style where the groups of plants need constant manipulation.

Looking back towards the house, the Mount Etna broom towers above red roses. Golden-leaved honey locust, *Gleditsia triacanthus* 'Sunburst', is a neighbour to the variegated holly, *Ilex × altaclarensis* 'Golden King'; salvias, alchemillas and hostas are grouped in broad sweeps towards the border's edge.

LEFT Pale yellow achilleas, pink-flowered diascias and geraniums are grouped in front of silvery santolinas and spiked-leaved irises. As well as growing a supply of annuals to enrich his colour schemes, Christopher Lloyd runs a commercial nursery and so often changes over perennial groups in the middle of summer, taking the early-flowerers for nursery division and growing-on, and replacing them with later-summer performers.

ABOVE The garden at Great Dixter, looking away from the house and main border (shown on the previous pages). The paved and mown terrace runs above the dry moat where wildflowers are naturalized and is linked with the orchard by Lutyens' broad projecting steps.

RIGHT ABOVE and BELOW Daisy-flowered *Erigeron karvinskianus* seeds in Lutyens' stonework where his dramatic concave and convex steps lead gently from the terrace below the house to the orchard. Mown grass unites terrace, steps and orchard, the smooth lawn contrasting with the long textured grass in the meadow, and the path beckoning invitingly.

FAR RIGHT Nathaniel Lloyd designed the octagonal pool in the sunken garden at Great Dixter in 1923. Wide stone paving surrounds the water and seedling *Acaena microphylla* grow in the pavement cracks. A yew archway leads to another garden compartment. The firm structure provides the perfect foil to Christopher Lloyd's informal planting style.

THE PATTERNED GARDEN

Plants as Decorative Elements · Hard & Soft Patterns

Kitchen Gardens · Informal Flower Patterns · Knot Gardens

The Parterre · The Maze · Topiary · Water Patterns

La Chèvre d'Or · An Enclosed Bruges Garden

Decoration in architecture is not a material part of the structure; similarly, in gardening, decorative beds or upright pieces of topiary may not be an essential part of a garden layout. They are ornamental devices designed to lighten or humanize a framework.

This chapter deals with patterns which are obviously decorative, and often of a scale that is most effective when viewed as a whole or from above. They range from the more complex, intricate designs of the historical knot garden, parterre or maze to simpler, more informal arrangements of different coloured foliage or flowers against a background of evergreen plants or brick or stone. Whether of plants or hard materials, or a combination of the two, such patterns are designed to make strong visual statements in contrast to the structural framework of a garden which is often hidden, or at least not immediately apparent. Many of the most successful patterned gardens contain elements which can be traced back to the first man-made gardens.

The patterned layout of the earliest paradise gardens of Persia evolved from enclosed, irrigated areas in which the symmetrical arrangement of water, trees and flowerbeds contrasted with the desert landscape beyond the perimeter. The garden's ordered pattern, usually the *chahar bagh* (where the garden was divided by water channels into four quarters), was the source of Persian carpet designs. The four rivers of life, based on man's progress between birth and death, met in the centre and ran in symmetrical channels. The gardens had raised pavilions which marked corners and often a central mausoleum from which the four rivers appeared to flow. From these buildings, rows of fruit trees, such as pomegranate, apricot and peach, and flowerbeds, arranged in perfectly symmetrical patterns, could be viewed. Broad-headed plane trees gave shade and contrasted dramatically with soaring vertical cypresses, the symbols of man's immortality.

The Persian garden was later adopted as a style by Islam and introduced into southern Europe by the Arabs and into India by the Moguls. In Moorish courtyard gardens, water channels often

ABOVE At Cranborne Manor in Dorset, an espaliered apple forms a free-standing vertical pattern and, from a design point of view, makes a strong architectural feature. Training fruit trees has been a practice since gardening first began: the French excel at intricate shapes while in England fruit trees are usually either fan-shaped, cordon-trained or espaliered. Espalier trees are often grown against warm walls which protect the blossom from late frosts and encourage the fruit to ripen early.

PREVIOUS PAGES: LEFT The vast terraced garden at Villandry in Touraine, France, was created by Dr Joachim Carvallo between 1906 and 1924 and is still maintained and cultivated by his grandson. On the lowest level, a vegetable garden or potager, of about 4000 square metres (1 acre), is divided into nine squares of different coloured foliage. Here, decorative ruby chard is shown alternating with squares of elegant cos lettuce leaves. Each square is enclosed by a low trellis work fence with rose-covered trellis arbours at every corner, coinciding with the intersection of the paths. All the main beds are edged with dwarf box hedging (see p. 105).

PREVIOUS PAGES: RIGHT At Howick Hall in Northumberland, rough grass is bright with naturalized tulips and drifts of daffodils. Planted like a wildflower meadow rather than massed for colour effect, the tulips remind one of the 'flowery meads' so often portrayed in religious paintings of the late Middle Ages. The spangled pattern and subtle colour markings of the tulip petals blend in the eye, a complete contrast to the elaborate discipline of the Villandry ornamental vegetable plots.

RIGHT At Levens Hall in Cumbria, yew and box are cut into fantastic shapes, reflecting light and shadow from their textured leaves. Some of the clipped specimens, which date from the end of the 17th century, are symbolic and linked to the history of the house. Probably of Dutch inspiration, this sort of topiary garden is rare. Box-edged beds frame the massive yew and smaller rounded or spiralling box shapes; in these, annuals of one colour, massed as a carpet of blue, make a perfect and simple setting.

flowed from a central pool, and pathways raised high above the flowerbeds allowed an unbroken view of the patterned planting.

The medieval *hortus conclusus* of Christian motivation was in spirit akin to the Persian paradise garden – a retreat from which the outside world was metaphorically excluded. Few records exist and medieval gardens are portrayed as having more form and discipline than they actually did. Paths, instead of rivers, mark out a pattern; raised beds and seats replace pavilions; rectangular and square beds are filled with herbs. Trellis work screens, covered in wild roses, honeysuckle and grapevines, separate areas or are shaped to form tunnels or arbours; low trellis edges the flowerbeds. Sometimes, alternate squares of turf and flowerbed make a strong chequered pattern. Even the 'flowery meads' – clover lawns spangled with a thousand various wildflowers – are arranged geometrically. In reality, such gardens were more likely to have been simply divided into square plots, in which essential culinary and medicinal herbs were carefully tended and fruit trees neatly trimmed into ornamental shapes.

The simple patterned layout of these medieval gardens was the inspiration for both the decorative vegetable 'potager', of which the French have made a feature, and the purely functional, traditional kitchen garden, where vegetables are grown in straight lines for convenience of cultivation and cropping. La Quintinie (1626-88) designed the famous *Potager du Roi* at Versailles for Louis XIV, and one at Sceaux for Colbert. Perhaps the best-known vegetable garden is at Villandry in France, of 17th-century inspiration.

The more intricate patterns of knot gardens, mazes, parterres and topiary shapes are decorative techniques related to particular historical periods. Today, from a purely technical point of view, formal patterned gardens such as these are easier to maintain than they were in the past. Modern herbicides and electric hedge cutters make this sort of gardening more labour-saving, for example, than informal borders with mixed planting. In the latter an annual reshuffling of plant masses, requiring a great deal of skill as well as hard work, is necessary to make a planting area look good all through a season.

Many contemporary gardeners dislike the idea of formality and regimentation that goes with the patterned style of gardening, feeling that there is little opportunity for personal expression and fearing that a formal layout, in which every plant has its designated role, may be static in effect. In fact, this is not necessarily so: box patterns can enclose flowerbeds where planting of various-sized perennials, bulbs or annuals can be as informal as in borders with irregular curves.

Many gardens, and certainly Tintinhull, depend for their success on an element of repetition in planting schemes or colour groups. At Tintinhull, grey foliage (in particular senecios and arte-misias) is repeated on many corners and in several of the garden compartments. The colour emphasis acts as a link, binding the design together as comprehensively as the continuous backing hedge. Effects are most restful if a pattern is repeated at least once. Similarly, tree and bush shapes should be complementary: rounded shapes provide an interesting contrast to vertical fastigiate forms, but too much variation can be distracting. Making a garden is like composing a painting in three dimensions: each garden view is a composition where colours and shapes together build up to a complete picture and where a recognizable pattern lends order and coherence to the overall design.

LEFT At Hestercombe in Somerset, Sir Edwin Lutyens, in partnership with Gertrude Jekyll, used the rough local stone for making elaborate paving. They worked together in the vernacular whenever possible, weaving stone and brick patterns of great delicacy, the textured surfaces a perfect accompaniment to the rich planting schemes. Here, the same stone has been used to line the pool.

BELOW In the courtyard at Cranborne Manor, Dorset, cobbles in diminishing sizes are arranged in overlapping concentric circles, their smooth, rounded shape and compact form creating a pleasing rippled effect. The cobble stones are set in a mixture of tightly rolled sand and loose cement, which is then watered to make it set, ensuring a firm foundation.

LEFT In the great vegetable garden at Villandry, a long, low border of chives of uniform colour and texture stands in striking contrast to an adjoining bed of bright, pink and white annuals. These long borders provide an outer edge to the rigid rectangular beds which lie within each square, as well as creating a linear perspective which serves to increase the feeling of distance.

LEFT Cabbages in staggered rows and a line of leeks contribute their own simple pattern at Tintinhull, where the kitchen garden remains strictly functional. Vegetables are sown or planted in rows at right angles to the main path, just as they have traditionally been planted since medieval times. The Tintinhull vegetable garden is in four sections with cross paths meeting at the centre. One, lined with catmint, stretches the length of the garden; the other, flanked with espalier pears, is edged with pink roses.

ABOVE Stone paving slabs set in gravel mark out a grid system for a new kitchen garden in the city of Atlanta, Georgia. Ryan Gainey, a garden designer, uses geometric patterns and clipped shapes not only in his ornamental garden but also in his vegetable patch, so that a formal theme runs throughout. Low box hedges and flowers edge massed plantings of lettuces. Standard fruit trees in pots accentuate the corners and can be moved to shelter during winter months.

LEFT Flanked by Irish yews, a stone pathway leading from the garden door at Barnsley House is planted with sun-loving helianthemums in pale mauve, pink, white and primrose to make a carpet of blending colour. This sort of informal pattern-making is like embroidery where woven threads harmonize to create an overall design. The heavy dark greens of the funereal yews (at the top of the picture of the Barnsley knot on p. 111) contrast in tone and weight with the delicate pastel tints.

KNOT GARDENS

By Tudor times, patterned knot gardens had become a common feature of garden design. A continuous band of interlacing, low-growing plants formed the outline to the pattern, which sometimes featured heraldic beasts shaped in sand but was more often a geometrical design within a square area. Based on embroidery 'over and under' work, plants of distinctive foliage colour and texture were used to fill the outer frame.

The earliest representation of a knot garden is in the *Hypnerotomachia Poliphili* published in 1499, where the interlaced outline is filled with flowers and herbs. In this book, woodcuts show other ingenious decorative embellishments, including a labyrinth, ornate topiary, a wood-trellised pergola and flowerbeds laid out in intricate patterns. The book was not adequately translated into English until the 18th century, but a French rendering of 1546, although not accurate, was of considerable influence on subsequent

garden style. Thyme and hyssop were first used for the low hedges, but by the 1600s box had become popular for its greater clarity of form. Inside the edging were native and exotic flowers: daffodils, fritillaries, hyacinths, tulips and anemones.

Knot gardens may consist of outlines of box, santolinas, rosemary, rue or germander, and contain inner planting of flowers or leaves of a particular colour. Small topiary specimens of spiralling box or holly give height and emphasis to the corners of a flat design (see also p. 121).

FAR LEFT In the 1960s at Cranborne Manor, Lady Salisbury laid out a Tudor knot garden on a flat area of lawn, sheltered by tall lime trees. In it she planted not only culinary and medicinal herbs but small tulips, violas and pinks which would have been known in the 17th century. Diamond- and square-shaped beds, all edged with low box, are arranged around a central circular bed. Domes, spirals and pyramids of box make vertical accents. The free planting style used to fill the geometric shapes gives a charmingly informal air to the structured layout of this garden.

LEFT At Barnsley House Rosemary Verey, the knowledgeable gardener and garden historian, has made a garden which reflects the architectural period of the late 17th-century house. The gardens, as they have developed over the last twenty years, are strongly structured, with an overall pattern of straight lines, cross axes and focal points, richly disguised by luxuriant and interesting planting. Mrs Verey also has a fine library of antiquarian garden books and the knot garden, about 5 × 8 metres (17 × 26 feet) in size, was adapted from a plan in a pattern book of the early 17th century. The lines of the design, which is set in pale gravel, are marked out in box and germander (*Teucrium chamaedrys*). Domes of evergreen *Phillyrea angustifolia* and variegated box, with double domes of holly at the corners, give height.

THE PARTERRE

The French parterre is an elaboration of the geometric knot garden (see p.110). Traditionally, parterres were invented by Claude Mollet in the 16th century for the Queen of France, Catherine de Medici, who missed the patterned layout of the Italian gardens. Early designs were disciplined and laid out on large flat areas below the house. Later, a succession of parterres, framed by thick woodland, would form long vistas stretching out into the distance. With time, designs were less geometric and featured freer scroll and feather patterns. These more intricate designs, known as *parterres de broderie*, were often of boxwood outlines containing gravel, sand or flowers.

In England and Holland, parterres were invariably box-edged patterns containing mown grass or, even more simply, patterns cut in turf and filled with coloured sand or gravel. Unfashionable in the 18th century, the parterre was revived in W. A. Nesfield's 19th-century designs for large-scale Italianate gardens featuring box-edged beds filled with coloured gravels. An example of his work remains in good order at Broughton Hall in Yorkshire.

Over the last twenty years, there has been a movement to re-create gardens within an historical context and many new box parterres have been designed to accompany period houses (see Hatfield House, p. 46). This sort of disciplined planting can be particularly effective in small gardens.

BELOW and RIGHT At La Garoupe on the Cap d'Antibes near Cannes, Mr Anthony Norman has laid out massed parterres of aromatic lavender, rosemary and santolinas. In the centre of each, pyramids of box surround elegant Italian urns.

Mr Norman's grandparents built the Italianate villa at La Garoupe at the turn of the century with elaborate, vast parterres on an Edwardian scale to match the style of the house. After the 1938-45 war, Mr Norman replaced the labour-intensive designs with this much simpler planting scheme.

Exotic planting is mainly near the house and in the centre of the garden, while near the perimeter native plants are permitted to encroach on the flowerbeds. Yuccas, American agaves and South African bulbs enjoy the favourable conditions. Pencil-slim cypresses line the lower terrace walk and rugged Aleppo pines grow by the sea shore.

FAR LEFT At the Château du Pontrancart near Dieppe, four parterres are laid out on the lawn above the moat. Silvery-leaved lavender, thyme and santolinas, grown as flat carpets for colour and texture effect, are all clipped to encourage dense leaf growth and a compact habit. Box has been used to edge and give definition to each elaborate shape. In the distance, yew hedges are arranged in a grid system and provide a dark background to flowerbeds designed for maximum colour in August and September, the only two months in which the Château is occupied.

LEFT The Garden of Hearts, adjoining the Van Buuren Museum in Brussels, was designed by René Pêchere for Madame Van Buuren and was completed in only five months, between autumn 1969 and spring 1970. The outline of the whole garden and each flowerbed is in the shape of a heart. Originally, the red flowers were roses but today begonias have taken their place. There is no precise interpretation of this garden but these words may give a clue: 'Secret garden of the heart, garden of secret hearts, Friend, it is for you to discover the garden of your heart.'

RIGHT ABOVE The gardens at Filoli, south of San Francisco, were laid out at the end of the 1914-18 war. They include a 6.5-hectare (16-acre) formal garden where annuals are bedded out inside a formal structure of walls and hedges. The white, red and yellow pansies cover the ground inside the lines of the rectangular box-edged beds, which provide a setting for flowers throughout the year in the mild Californian climate.

RIGHT BELOW Next to the rectangular beds, red and mauve pansies carpet the ground right up to the tree trunk inside swirling hedges of clipped box. The vivid masses of colour, separated by bands of green, remain clearly distinct rather than mingling and blending in the eye.

RIGHT The planting scheme in this Belgian garden (see p. 94) is typical of those designed by Jacques Wirtz. Box-edged beds, arranged geometrically, are used to contain the very strong forms of upward and outward-growing plants, which literally flow over the edges. Such a scheme may make maintenance difficult but the composition is magical. Tall, creamy spires of *Aruncus dioicus*, outlined against a high background hedge, arch over hostas, astrantias, alchemillas and astilbes – all plants which revel in light shade. Beyond the taller hedges lies a Catalpa garden and a swimming pool.

THE MAZE

The maze or labyrinth was first used in garden design in the 15th century. The two terms seem almost interchangeable, although some writers insist that mazes refer specifically to those layouts in which hedges are used to mark out a confusing pattern, while the labyrinth, having its origins in Greek mythology, refers to any symbolic, organized pattern which contains a puzzle. The labyrinth originally represented the tortuous windings of the Minotaur at Knossos, but later, with Christianity, it came to be symbolic of man's journey through the hazards of life on earth. A water labyrinth is illustrated in *Hypnerotomachia Poliphili* (see p. 110). With the addition of astrological signs – circles and squares representing heaven and earth respectively – the labyrinth became the basis for intricate garden patterns, perhaps the historical inspiration for knot gardens and the later box-edged parterres and *broderies*.

The first mazes were low-cut, in stone, rock or turf and it was not until the end of the 17th century that they were made of plants grown above head height in order to deliberately confuse and also to amuse. Charles Perrault laid out a sculpture maze at Versailles where statues linked by alleys of green plants covered a vast area stretching 750 metres (2460 feet). This maze was destroyed in 1784. The best-known maze in England is that in yew at Hampton Court, first planted in 1690; a copy of its pattern in beech was made at Tatton Park in Edwardian times. At Glendurgan in Cornwall a cherry laurel maze, designed by Alfred Fox in 1833, lies on a steep slope. Today, some recently restored Tudor gardens, such as the one in front of the Old Palace at Hatfield (see p. 46) include a maze in low-cut box.

LEFT ABOVE The modern turf maze at Greys Court, near Henley-on-Thames, represents the path of life (the pilgrimage from birth to death, judgment and salvation). The 'Chemin de Jerusalem', the pilgrims' path to the Holy Land, is marked out by the brick pattern in a series of concentric rings just below the level of the turf. Although the pattern is only 25 metres (82 feet) across, the path winds for over 400 metres (three-quarters of a mile) to a central stone. The overall design represents the Crown of Thorns.

LEFT BELOW René Pêchere designed the Labyrinth Garden near the Garden of Hearts (see p. 114). On an unpromising sloping site, Pêchere carved out the winding labyrinth using more than 300 yews. The complex pattern, which represents Alice van Buuren's idealization of the Song of Solomon, is enhanced by sculptures set in circles of yew. The cedar tree, situated to one side, is the central goal. To reach it the path winds and twists for 190 metres (620 feet) – provided no wrong turns are taken.

ABOVE This maze was designed by the Italian landscape artist, Pietro Porcinai (1910-86), in the grounds of Villa il Roseto, a Medici villa at Arcetri in the hills just outside Florence. In Porcinai's designs, each object is designed to stimulate the imagination, its exact meaning less important than its immediate provocative quality. Open and closed patterns in whole or part circles of grass and paving deliberately confuse the mind. At the centre, shown here in the foreground, a tightly clipped hedge conceals steep descending steps that lead to an underground garage.

TOPIARY

Plants have been cut into ornamental shapes at least since the time of Pliny the Younger who cut box in many strange ways, some spelling out his gardener's name. Originally *topiaria opera* meant any kind of ornamental gardening, but gradually topiary has come to have a more specific reference to clipping and shaping living plants. During the Middle Ages, plants were cut simply, with fruit trees either pleached or espaliered to produce crops within a restricted space, but after the publication of *Hypnerotomachia Poliphili* (see p. 110), elaborate topiary became a fashion in garden design. In Renaissance Italy and in the rest of Europe during the 16th and 17th centuries, almost any plant was subjected to the shears – holly, yew, box, bay, laurel, *Phillyrea* and *Rhamnus* were among the most popular for this treatment. By the middle of the 18th century, artificiality in garden design was scorned and considered bad taste, but by the end of the 19th century topiary was back in vogue again.

Today, like the box-edged bed or box parterre, topiary features are again in demand, both for restorations of period gardens and new garden-making. In even a small garden, the decorative quality and strong outlines of topiary add extra dimension and depth and make a perfect foil to free plant forms and leaf shapes or to a level lawn.

LEFT At the Belvedere at Laeken on the outskirts of Brussels, Arabella Lennox-Boyd has designed a formal garden to sit on a flat area in front of the 19th-century palace. A strictly symmetrical pattern of clipped yew hedging and topiary shapes appears, at first glance, to be in striking contrast to the background of flowering trees in the woodland beyond the garden boundaries. A close look reveals a similarity in form between the vertical hornbeam and yew shapes and the tall poplars and church spire in the distance. Topiary is most successful when, as here, it has some visible link with the house or surrounding landscape, rather than being entirely fanciful.

ABOVE In a secret corner of this small London garden, spirals of box are set at corners of a rectangular bed, edged with a low outer hedge of plain green box and an inner higher hedge of variegated box. *Santolina* and lavender are planted within, around the central spiral. Vertical and horizontal symmetrical shapes are used to contrast with the freer planting in the border at the back, bringing a sense of order to the garden. The topiary shapes and low clipped hedging have been used to create the impression of 'a garden within a garden'.

WATER PATTERNS

Water was an integral part of the patterned layout of the earliest-known gardens, set in the arid deserts of Persia (see p. 102). In these gardens, channels of moving water represented the passage of time, while cubic and rectangular-shaped pools symbolized stability.

Pools, fountains and the horizontal and vertical patterns they create have always been a central feature of garden design, often within an ornamental framework of tiles, stones and bricks. In Roman times, Hadrian's villa was surrounded by canals and pools, while at the 16th-century Villa d'Este, a hundred fountains lined the side of a single alley. Cascades and practical water jokes were a recurring feature in 17th-century Italian gardens. In France, at about the same time, water was used on a massive scale: Le Nôtre manipulated the water levels of ornamental pools, cleverly distorting perspective so that dimensions expanded, even doubling in length. The 16th-century water parterre designed by Vignola at the Villa Lante, Bagnaia, Italy, the more recently created parterre at Villa La Gamberaia (see pp. 30-31) and Achille Duchêne's design for Blenheim Palace are all examples of water patterns in the grandest style.

LEFT The Blenheim water parterre, laid out by Achille Duchêne for the ninth Duke of Marlborough, closely resembles the design for the *parterre d'eau* at Versailles. After raising the surrounding water level and enlarging the lake in the 1760s, 'Capability' Brown had left this western side of the palace as a green lawn. So it remained until 1925, when Duchêne set out the two terraces and designed the curving water basins and scrolled patterns of low box hedging set in gravel panels. Fountain jets give vertical emphasis and enliven the smooth water surface. The parterre is on a vast scale and was designed to be admired from the windows above.

ABOVE At Bowood in Wiltshire, Charles Hamilton, the owner and maker of the gardens at Painshill, designed a cascade in 1785. Falling over three stepped levels of natural-looking rock facing, the water curtains make a dramatic vertical pattern. Situated at the approach to 'Capability' Brown's lake, the cascades are based on a painting by Gaspard Poussin. A grotto tunnel, built by Josiah Lane, is hidden underneath the waterfall. The sound and movement of the water recall a mountain river, a complete contrast to the geometric water forms of the Blenheim parterre, opposite.

LA CHÈVRE D'OR

The garden at La Chèvre d'Or, near Biot in the south of France, demonstrates clearly how plants used as architectural features can provide both the basic structure and the ornamental details in garden design. The late Madame Champin made a garden for all seasons in which decorative features are enhanced by colour, with flowering shrubs, climbers and bulbs performing throughout the year. She began the garden over forty years ago when, using the existing olive groves and horizontal terraces, she planted pines and tall Italian cypresses, grouped as focal points or arranged linearly along the edge of paths. Stone walls were used to reinforce the terraces: on one, clipped and pleached olive trees form a horizontal raised hedge; on another, the silver-leafed palm *Erythea armata* flourishes. Taking advantage of the Riviera climate, Madame Champin added exotics which make the garden as interesting for the plantsman as many botanic collections. Against the evergreen background, bushes of blue-flowered *Ceanothus*, cascading mauve and white wisterias and white-flowered roses, climbing into old olive trees, have grown to giant proportions. Nearer ground level, tender Asiatic buddleias, spikes of *Echium*, glaucous-leaved *Melianthus major* from South Africa and a collection of Mexican salvias add colour and interest. In the cobbled courtyard by the house, night-flowering *Cestrum nocturnum* fills the air with fragrance.

LEFT Semi-circles of box are used to make a repetitive serpentine pattern along the upper edge of the main lawn at La Chèvre d'Or. Ornamental terracotta pots on plinths and lemon trees alternate within the curves of the box hedge. The pots were originally planted with tender myrtles, the native *Myrtus communis*, but now, after several severe winters, they are filled with hardier evergreens such as standard Portuguese laurel, *Prunus lusitanica*.

RIGHT Madame Champin allowed the basic pattern of olive terraces, typical of the Riviera hillsides, to dictate the garden framework. Their horizontal lines make a contrast to the soaring Italian cypresses which she added for wind protection and to give the garden a sense of seclusion. On the lower lawn, there is no flower colour to distract from the design; instead, a composition of greens and greys contributes muted colour to architectural form, producing a well-balanced picture. In the foreground, a broad, shallow pool and central fountain add sound and movement.

LEFT Evergreen leaves provide an all-season backdrop to more fleeting colour incidents, such as the pergolas hung with wisteria – a regular feature at La Chèvre d'Or. Colourful in spring, they create refreshingly cool walks and sitting places in summer. Hot summers ripen the wood and mild rainy winters promote growth, which encourages climbers to perform superbly. The terraces also offer well-drained, warm sites for a variety of tender shrubs and bulbs.

RIGHT White roses cascade through an olive tree overlooking a modernistic chequerboard design of silver-leaved *Santolina* set in a bed of gravel. The pergola helps to frame the striking flat design. The long pendulous racemes of mauve wisteria echo the line of cypresses and emphasize the falling rose branches and slope of the bank.

AN ENCLOSED BRUGES GARDEN

Formal patterned planting schemes, because of their historical association, are often considered suitable only for grand gardens; in fact, most of these intricate geometric designs are especially effective when translated into a more modest scale.

This garden in the heart of the Belgian city of Bruges, designed by André van Wassenhove, has a maze-like quality of surprise. But, far from being confusing, the layout of low brick walls and hedges set in brick paving, provides a logical pattern of separate yet interlinked compartments which makes this enclosed garden seem much larger than it is. The width of each path and hedge and the height of the walls are carefully related to the whole: taller hedges would crowd the garden, lower dwarf hedging would turn the pattern into a parterre. The design allows freedom of movement between each area; its unity creates a perfect blend of intimacy and spaciousness. The plants are chosen for the quality of their foliage; wall-clinging creepers, forms of *Parthenocissus*, thrive in this garden and give rich autumn colour.

LEFT The success of this enclosed garden lies in the well-thought out combination of bricks and paving which set off a variety of foliage textures and hues. Much of the garden is overshadowed by high walls and, as here, it is often better to cover horizontal surfaces with low-maintenance hard materials than attempt to grow grass in shade.

ABOVE and RIGHT Box hedges are neatly trimmed to the same height as the low brick walls, breaks in their pattern inviting access. Broad-headed mulberries and apple trees give height and mask buildings, yet relate in scale to the geometric layout, while low-growing shade-tolerant perennials thrive under their spreading branches in the open rectangular beds.

THE MORE NATURAL GARDEN

Informal Planting . Robinsonian Planting

Groundcover . Shrub Borders . Woodland

Self-seeding Plants . Water . The 'New Style'

East Lambrook . Longstock Water Gardens

The very essence of 'natural' gardening is the apparent freedom of plants to shape a garden picture, whether it is a park, plantsman's woodland, the outer fringes of a country garden or a small suburban garden where planting disciplines can be relaxed to convey an unplanned atmosphere. The more natural garden has seemingly casual planting themes where individual plants or groups of plants are encouraged to behave and flourish as if put there by nature. In reality it should be as carefully planned and executed as any formal pattern and actually requires more aesthetic and horticultural skill. This approach to gardening is perhaps the most popular of all garden styles but is certainly that which is the least understood and least well executed.

The success of the great English 18th-century landscape (see p. 8) depended on its appearance of having evolved from nature. Its shaping required the changing of land contours and grouping of trees to influence the whole landscape. In its translation as a style to other countries and also in the use of its principles in laying out quite small gardens, it has not always been successful. During the 19th century attempts to turn formal European gardens, of Italian or French influence, into so-called English gardens, where winding paths curve between tree or shrub specimens, planted in grass, were and are seldom satisfying. In England, although often the 18th-century parkland survived, vast bedding schemes and monumental Italianate gardens became fashionable during the succeeding century; it remained for William Robinson writing in the 1880s to redirect the mainstream of English gardening style. In *The Wild Garden* (1881) he advised the use of hardy native and exotic plants in natural association in woodland or streamside settings where they would thrive and spread, a theme which is variously interpreted today in both large and small gardens. He recommended 'naturalising innumerable beautiful natives of many regions of the earth' in conditions approximating to their native habitat. To the Victorians, accustomed to bedding-out of annuals twice yearly for ostentatious display, this was a revolutionary concept.

In the new 'wild' gardening single plants, although allowed freedom to develop, should never draw attention to themselves but should blend harmoniously into an overall scheme. For Robinson this style was 'best explained by the winter aconite flowering under a grove of naked trees in February; by the Snowflake growing abundantly in meadows by the Thames side . . . and by the Apennine anemone staining an English wood blue before the blooming of our blue bells'. His ideas were equally useful in the development of the plantsman's woodland. By the last years of the 19th century new introductions from Asia were added to those already available; it was no longer possible to incorporate these exotic trees and shrubs in any existing and traditional layout. Each plant needed to be given a suitable site and geometric or symmetrical planting schemes could not accommodate growing and spreading branches which quickly altered the balance of a scheme. Woodland gardening, as a craft, must imply a degree of naturalism; its spirit must not be defined by artificial laws. Yet a woodland, just like a garden, must have design coherence. Observation and experience of plant growth and behaviour become as important as plant association and relevant scale. The woodland garden becomes an idealized 'wilderness' – but one in which man, not nature, is firmly in control.

Robinson's advice for more natural gardening is variously interpreted today; it is useful for any size of garden. Its 'rules' are as applicable to a shrub border, to a corner in a small garden overshadowed by overhead trees and to the planting round the banks of an artificial pond as they are to the grander properties about which he originally wrote. Much of his advice was confirmed by Gertrude Jekyll's gardening writing and practice. She stressed the importance in a country garden of using native shrubs and plants at its perimeter, so allowing a garden to merge naturally into the countryside beyond. At Munstead Wood she planted hollies and junipers where the garden drifted into the Surrey woodland. She sounded a warning note: 'Wild gardening should never look like garden gardening, or, as it so sadly often does, like garden plants gone astray'.

PREVIOUS PAGES: LEFT Planting round a pond at Saling Hall in Essex shows how effectively sturdy foliage plants can cover the soil, reducing garden maintenance to a minimum. The success of this scheme depends, not on the seasonal flower colour, but on the varied greens and textures of the foliage. The leaves of American skunk cabbage, *Lysichiton americanum*, shuttlecock ferns, *Matteuccia struthiopteris*, hostas and lady's mantle, *Alchemilla mollis*, combine to create luxuriant cover.

PREVIOUS PAGES: RIGHT The graceful *Selinum tenuifolium* from the Himalayas has lacy white flower umbels above very finely cut leaves. E. A. Bowles called it 'the most beautiful of all fern-leaved plants'. Flowering in August after the common cow-parsley is over, it is at its best in a natural setting.

FAR LEFT Successful plant association depends not only on artistic grouping for colour and shape but also on combinations of plants which thrive in similar conditions. In this border, evergreen shrubs with good form and foliage provide a frame on which late summer-flowering clematis can climb.

LEFT At the Priory, Kemerton, Gloucestershire, a double border, hidden from immediate view, is filled with flowering shrubs and low-growing perennials which flow over the edges of the central paving stones, uniting the two beds which are actually designed as one border. The central well of closely packed plants is backed by tall shrubs which give structure and increase the feeling of seclusion.

LEFT In Mr H. Thomas Halloway's garden at Deerfield, Pennsylvania, mid-century lilies have naturalized beside a stream. The essence of this relaxed style lies in using the natural vegetation, and only adding plants which fit visually into the landscape. In the rich acid leaf mould and light shade cast by the native tulip trees (*Liriodendron tulipifera*) in this valley garden, American woodland shrubs and some exotic introductions thrive with the lilies. Shrubs as well as bulbs and perennials can be 'naturalized' in suitable conditions.

ABOVE At Anne's Grove in the mild climate of County Cork in Eire, foliage plants grow quickly in rich alluvial soil. At the water's edge, the striking, sculptural leaves of giant *Gunnera* are framed by fine trees. The Anne's Grove woodland and water gardens are supreme examples of Robinsonian precepts. Under the branches of native and exotic trees and shrubs, hardy low-growing perennials make a perfect natural cover.

ABOVE At Vann near Hambledon, Surrey, Gertrude Jekyll advised on the water garden. The spirit of the whole garden expresses her philosophy; much of the original planting survives. Like Robinson, Miss Jekyll loved to naturalize hardy plants and bulbs in suitable conditions: the snake's head fritillary, *Fritillaria meleagris*, and drifts of narcissi thrive in rough grass and have spread along the edge of the lake. Informal planting of hardy bulbs can best be achieved by studying natural groupings of wildflowers in woods, copses, heaths and meadows.

RIGHT Beside a pond in Jersey in the Channel Islands, groups of the hardy arum, *Zantedeschia aethiopica*, spread along the bank, softening the water's edge. As in all Robinsonian-style gardening, the best and most natural effects are gained by using few rather than many different plant types. In waterside planting schemes, it is important to ensure that an adequate supply of water is available for plant roots in times of drought.

The two commonly held assumptions about 'natural' gardening are that, as a style, it is easy to plant for aesthetic effect and that it is synonymous with very little work. In fact these 'wild' gardens need to be as carefully composed as an artist's paints on a canvas, with an eye to heights, shapes, density and colour, with the added complications of working in three dimensions and using living and growing plants as tools, plants which are to be allowed to realise their full potential. Because there are no exact rules to follow, the gardener, while using horticultural knowledge to make plants appear at home in their setting, has to allow for their different rates of growth and changing aspect over the future years. This style of gardening is only labour-saving if a scheme reflects a deep understanding of all these factors.

A wide variety of planting themes can be included under the embrasive title of 'natural' gardening. All of them should convey an atmosphere of relaxed planting, effects which to some degree disguise the existence of a coherent overall master plan. A completely natural garden may be woodland, meadow or streamside where only native trees, shrubs and wildflowers are permitted. Although hardly gardens in the sense in which we normally use the term, these sanctuaries for flora (and consequently fauna) have become necessary where man has either wantonly or deliberately destroyed natural habitats through industrial or urban pollution. At the opposite end of the garden scale, with no underlying ecological significance, is a good shrub border, where woody plants grow in harmony and compose a balanced picture. Between the shrubs low-growing foliage plants, mainly perennials, can be massed as groundcover. Arranged in natural-looking drifts these completely carpet bare soil and allow no light or space for weed germination.

By tradition, grass is the most popular form of groundcover; it can be cut at different heights to provide variable textures and visual interest. Areas of longer grass can be shaped either to match overhead canopies of nearby trees or the contours of a slope. Smooth lawn, cut on average once a week during the summer, can have its area extended by directional pathways through longer grass which is cut monthly, or if naturalized with bulbs and perennials, only cut after seeds ripen in July and August. Shrubberies underplanted with perennial groundcovers can have their edges and ground shape defined by mown grass.

All but the most strict garden patterns benefit from some sort of free association, as long as size and scale relationships are kept in balance both for individual themes and for the overall garden picture. The formal garden, with modern low-maintenance techniques, is easy gardening; plants are arranged and tamed according to a rule book. The informal naturalistic theme may appear simple but its success depends on frequent decision-making and horticultural skill which usually come only from experience.

ABOVE When trees and shrubs are involved, aesthetic judgments and planning must make allowances for the time it takes each specimen to reach maturity. At the Dower House at Boughton House in Northamptonshire, the late Sir David Scott collected trees and shrubs in an 8000-square metre (2-acre) area, surrounded on three sides by mature woodland. Each specimen was given a site suited to its needs and where it could be seen to best advantage. Planting continued for forty years and today there are as many as eighty well-stocked island beds containing an impressive range of woody plants, under which shade-loving perennials and bulbs have spread to smother the soil. Valerie Finnis (Lady Scott), Sir David's second wife, has further enriched the woodland beds with uncommon low-growing plants.

RIGHT At Hidcote, Lawrence Johnston's planning combines a recognizable formality of structure in the main garden with more natural planting schemes in hidden areas. On the sloping banks of a stream, plants are encouraged to spread and mass as they would in nature. Shuttlecock ferns, *Matteucia struthiopteris*, line the edge of a path, displaying their fresh green fronds in early summer. Behind, the invasive comfrey, *Symphytum grandiflorum*, with coarse green leaves and nodding tubular flowers, suppresses all weeds. Both these plants thrive in half-shade and cool moist soil.

GROUNDCOVER

There are many plants which, although they do not make such a satisfying sward or walking surface, are much less labour intensive than grass and, spreading easily, give a natural carpeted effect massed below trees and shrubs and in open areas of the garden.

The choice of plants for groundcover depends essentially on scale, not only of the whole garden but of each area under consideration and the heights and spread of the taller trees and shrubs.

The invasive *Rubus tricolor* with shining leaves and reddish stems, *Gaultheria shallon* which thrives in acid soil, *Hypericum calycinum*, the well-known St John's Wort, and green or variegated forms of *Vinca major* and *V. minor* with single or double flowers in white, blue or purple, are all suckering evergreen shrubs which are admirable for covering quite large areas. Needing little maintenance, they are particularly suitable for steep banks and inaccessible areas; on flatter ground, their spread can be controlled by having mown grass paths edging the planting areas. Horizontal branching junipers and heathers (there are heathers for both acid and alkaline soil) will establish themselves as impenetrable groundcover but, vulnerable to adjacent mowing, they must be trimmed by hand. Green or variegated ivies and *Pachysandra terminalis* are more ground-hugging and, once well-established, need less attention than almost any other evergreen.

Many herbaceous plants are also effective for groundcover although they need planting in greater density than shrubs and have to be handweeded until established and matted together. Evergreen perennials such as *Ajuga*, some species of *Epimedium*, comfrey, lamiums, and the sweet-scented woodland violet will tolerate most soil conditions and thrive in shade. The deciduous perennials, such as hostas, *Alchemilla mollis*, pulmonarias, omphalodes and the blue-flowered *Brunnera macrophylla* all seed and spread to make natural-looking, close-growing drifts in light shade on the fringe of shrubberies, effectively preventing weed germination. *Trachystemon orientalis* needs more space to develop but its coarse, hairy leaves are particularly handsome.

This type of natural, low-level planting scheme need not be confined to woodland or shady areas. Spreading plants such as silvery-leaved snow-in-summer, *Cerastium tomentosum*, *Stachys byzantina*, *Anaphilis* and herbaceous artemisias all thrive in well-drained soil and full sun and can be encouraged to make abstract shapes, falling over stone edges or low walls. Blue campanulas and bronze-leaved violas seed in dry-stone walling, while alpine strawberries carpet rose-beds.

LEFT In the depths of the woodland garden at Royaumont in the Ile de France, a stone-edged bed is planted with rippling waves of *Hosta undulata*. Flanked with mown grass, the rich green twisted leaves centrally striped in cream and spikes of pale lilac flowers, reflect light as well as suppressing weeds. One grand effect such as this is more worthwhile than a display of individual specimen plants.

LEFT BELOW The pinkish foliage of *Ajuga reptans* 'Variegata' is useful beneath shrubs and roses in sun or shade. Although not invasive, this bugle, with bright blue flowers in early summer, is easy to establish.

BELOW The common fennel, *Foeniculum vulgare*, is highly decorative with umbels of small golden flowers on strong polished, bamboo-like stems. It is a strong grower and will seed prolifically. Pink-flowered *Phuopsis stylosa* spreads at its feet, making weed-resistant cover. To its right is a hazy cloud of sea lavender, blue-flowered *Limonium latifolium*.

RIGHT In spring, flowering bulbs set in rough grass make a tapestry under white cherry blossom in a garden at Klampenborg, Denmark. The earliest flowerers such as aconites, scillas and crocus can be grown in conventionally mown lawn as their leaves die down by the end of March. Daffodils and tulips perform later and mowing must be postponed for at least six weeks after flowering to allow the bulbs to absorb nutrients from the foliage. Highly bred tulips seldom 'naturalize' in rough grass and each year develop smaller flowerheads, which often makes them more attractive in an informal setting.

RIGHT At Kerdalo in Brittany, groups of woody and herbaceous plants are woven together in complementary drifts of flower and foliage colour. There is no rule book for this sort of gardening; its success depends on artistic judgment and a knowledge of how plants grow and change over the years as well as in one growing season. The shrubs have permanent sites while the herbaceous plants, both perennials and biennials, may need thinning out and replanting to ensure that a balance of form and colour is maintained.

FAR RIGHT At the Old Rectory near Farnborough, Berkshire, shrub roses arch over clumps of herbaceous geraniums and *Alchemilla*. The straight edges of the gravel path are disguised by cascading flowers and leaves, giving a pleasantly informal air to the garden layout. Most perennials will thrive and flower under rose bushes which only cast light shade but more vigorous spreading groundcover could damage the roses.

SHRUB BORDERS

Any hardy shrub border, whether near the house or at the garden's edge, will have a definite contained area. The low-growing plants accompanying the shrubs may be perennials such as hostas, rodgersias, day-lilies, *Acanthus* or tight mats of *Ajuga* or *Symphytum*. Their prime visual qualification is their ornamental leaf value rather than their more fleeting flowers, while their ground-covering ability reduces the amount of weeding required.

A bed or border where height is given by deciduous shrubs which come into leaf late in spring is a perfect site for the smaller woodland plants, both bulbs and perennials, which flower early and will tolerate shade throughout the summer. Scillas, chionodoxas, wood anemones, Apennine anemones, erythroniums and trilliums can all be allowed to spread in unplanned carpets. Clumps of hardy later-flowering bulbs can also be encouraged, especially when, like lilies, they thrive under the shelter of overhead leaves. Availability of time and labour will decide whether or not perennials and bulbs are occasionally divided or renewed to ensure better flowering performance.

Maintenance of this sort of border consists of pruning shrubs, once after flowering to remove flowering shoots and judiciously in winter to keep the composition in balance. Herbaceous perennials are attractive as they fade to brown and gold in early winter; they can have their flowering stems and dead leaves removed just once a year. Some gardeners do this in autumn and use a mulch to cover any bare earth between the plants while the ground is still warm. Others leave all cutting down until early spring, usually applying a mulch while the water table remains high to conserve moisture during the summer months. If the border has been well planned, all the plants will have grown together after a few years.

WOODLAND

Woodland gardens were first started as plant collections. Existing tree planting, when thinned out, often provided the perfect setting for many rhododendrons and other new woody plants introduced in the 19th century. Elsewhere, trees had first to be established to give protection, especially in those wind-swept sea-coast gardens where mild temperatures and humidity permitted experiment with tender southern hemisphere plants. At first there was little attempt to arrange plants in aesthetically pleasing groups; each specimen was given a suitable growing situation and was to be seen and admired as an individual plant. Gradually, more pleasing compositions were attempted; the art of woodland gardening developed as areas of dense shade were interrupted by open glades of sunlight.

Woodland plants are chosen and grouped for their form and foliage and in particular for their autumn colours, as well as for flowers and fruit. Planting is in layers; trees and tall shrubs shelter lower-growing shrubs and these in turn give protection to drifts of bulbs and shade-loving perennials. On alkaline soil, fallen leaves provide a natural mulch which tends to make the top layer of soil more acidic. It is the smaller plants, under the tiers of mainly deciduous trees and shrubs, which particularly enhance the 'natural' atmosphere. Planted according to Robinsonian principles, hardy native and foreign plants, which are often self-seeding, spread in shade or on the more open fringes of the woodland.

LEFT The gorge in the Glen garden at Crarae in Argyll is thickly planted with azaleas, *Hamamelis*, *Disanthus cercidifolius* and more rhododendrons. When Sir George Campbell first started to garden here in 1925, the steep banks of the glen were dense scrub of native birch, alder, oak, rowan and hazel. He used the dramatic landscape as his planting canvas and today the colours and textures of flowers, fruits and foliage in their respective seasons are a tribute to his artist's perception and the careful planning which he initiated over sixty years ago. Exotic and native trees, sometimes from the same genera, are grouped up the sides of the glen to provide shade and protection to the understorey of shrubs which need woodland conditions. Oak, birch, acers, *Sorbus*, tall conifers and *Eucalyptus* frame groups of rhododendrons, eucryphias, magnolias and many South American and Australasian woody plants which thrive in these favourable microclimatic conditions.

LEFT In the wood at Knightshayes, Devon, white foxgloves of the *Digitalis* 'Excelsior' strain have been encouraged to seed in woodland beds. Simple plants, used effectively, can be of more importance in creating a distinct atmosphere than exotic rarities. By midsummer when much of this part of the garden is green, the stately white foxgloves glow in the half-shade of the mature trees.

The style of woodland gardening is essentially informal; paths follow the natural contours and routes are determined by the overhead tree canopies.

BELOW At Tintinhull in Somerset, the wild English primrose (*Primula vulgaris*) flowers beside another European native, the snake's head fritillary (*Fritillaria meleagris*). In many gardens, primroses, although charming in spring, can quickly become an invasive weed and need restricting to banks and rougher areas. The fritillaries also seed prolifically; they flourish in damp meadows but will flower and multiply even in dry shady areas.

SELF-SEEDING PLANTS

In almost all gardens there are areas where certain plants, especially annuals and biennials, can be left to seed and flower *in situ*. These 'seeders' will scatter themselves in a bed or border, choosing any spot where soil is temporarily vacant and where there is enough overhead light for there to be successful germination and development. Time and labour can be saved by allowing these plants to seed naturally; some control can always be exercised if too many seedlings appear.

Even in traditional flower borders plants can be encouraged to self-seed to make colourful groups. This sort of relaxed informality is not only labour saving, but illuminates the whole conception of the 'wild' garden. Plants should grow where they flourish and are at home with their neighbours.

Biennials, such as spring-flowering white and mauve honesty (*Lunaria annua*), and a form with variegated leaves, love to seed in drifts through a border and are especially useful in shade. A good strain of forget-me-nots seldom disappears from a garden. Tall verbascums (forms of *Verbascum vernale, V. chaixii* or *V. phoeniceum*) and oenotheras (*Oenothera biennis*), small violas and primroses, eryngiums with thistle flowers and woodland foxgloves can all be encouraged to give a slightly unplanned 'natural' look to a garden. Of the latter there are several species with a range of flower colours all of which come true from seed. *Digitalis purpurea* has a white-flowered variant, *D. grandiflora* has greenish-cream flower-heads, *D. ferruginea* is bronze and *D. lutea* has narrow spires of pale yellow.

Opium poppies, *Nigella* and tender *Verbena bonariensis* can be allowed to seed naturally.

LEFT A border at Pusey House in which annuals such as opium and Iceland poppies look at home between clumps of conventional border plants. Unwanted extra seedlings can easily be eradicated after they germinate the following spring.

BELOW In Mr John Cavanagh's London garden, designed by Mr Brian Cox, giant *Gunnera* leaves spread over the edge of a pool. The stones, smoothed and surrounded by water, together with an overall economy in the use of plant colour and materials, achieve the restrained effect of a Japanese garden. The straight edge of the pool is formal but the jungle-like planting and casual drifts of stone give a natural look. The small-leaved Curse of Corsica, *Soleirolia soleirolii*, is moss-like and clings to stone or any similar surface.

RIGHT In a remote valley at Ockley near Dorking, Surrey, landscape designer Anthony Paul and Hannah Peschar have created a natural water garden framed by willows and poplars. It is an oasis of cool greens, where drifts of foliage of exotic and native moisture-loving plants make a foil to soaring modern sculptures. The emphasis in planting is on leaf shapes and texture rather than vivid colour which would only prove a distraction.

WATER

It is the natural planting scheme round a pond, particularly a small modern one with artificial lining, which is most difficult and demanding to design and maintain. This sort of natural looking water feature needs to be sited where the presence of water should seem inevitable and not in the middle of a lawn or at the top of a garden slope.

The pond edges should assume natural contours. They are concealed with soil and plants in drifts which creep up to drier areas and spread down into the water. Ledges, set at different levels for pots of true aquatics, are easily provided. The real problem is keeping adjacent soil damp enough to provide suitable conditions for the moisture-loving plants which are the glory of the water garden.

A natural pool edge supports the lush summer-growth of many foliage plants and flowering perennials which give colour throughout the season. Rheums, rodgersias, sedges, peltiphyllums, irises and *Gunnera* all have outstanding leaf form and texture. There are primulas and astilbes that flower through almost all the summer; their range will depend on the relative acidity or alkalinity of the soil.

In an artificial pool, traditional plants will not thrive unless the lining material is perforated to ensure that adequate moisture reaches the roots of the plants. It may be easier to set up a trickle system to do this as all pond-side planting can be affected by periods of drought. The alternative is to choose plants such as green-leaved, lush-looking *Acanthus, Agapanthus* and hostas which are not so fussy about damp and yet, with large textured leaves, fit into a waterside picture; drought-loving plants, with grey and silver leaves, look inappropriate round a pool.

LEFT, ABOVE and BELOW In Dr Harris' garden in Maryland, Baltimore, chocolate-brown rudbeckias beside pale-foliaged grass stems are backed by taller *Miscanthus*; translucent plumes of *Pennisetum alopecuroides* shine in sunlight.

ABOVE and ABOVE RIGHT *Astilbe* heads and contrasting grassy foliage shapes make a composition for all seasons, spilling over and softening hard walking surfaces in another garden in Baltimore.

THE 'NEW STYLE'

Oehme, Van Sweden, the landscape architects based in Washington DC, have inspired an exciting new style of 'natural' gardening both in private gardens and public places. Broad sweeps of perennials, grasses and other hardy herbaceous plants, with attractive form and strong foliage shapes and flowerheads provide interest almost through the year. This concept is directly opposed to traditional planting of heavy and static evergreen shrubs; instead, a few trees with delicate foliage, bamboos and tall *Miscanthus* grass provide vertical accents, and, importantly, move and rustle in the lightest breeze. Grasses (*Pennisetum* and *Calamagrostis*) and sedges (*Deschampsia* and *Carex*) are grouped to complement clumps of perennials: yellow coneflowers (forms of *Rudbeckia fulgida*) with brown heads in autumn, lavenders, sedums (*Sedum* 'Ruby Glow' and *S. spectabile* 'Autumn Joy') and ceratostigmas (with bronze stems in winter). These attractive knee-height groups are matched with massed low planting: ajugas, asarums, sweet-scented *Galium odoratum*, lamiums, and *Stachys byzantina* carpet the ground between the swaying grasses and swathes of flower stems as well as under the tree canopies. Tulips, used for spring effects, have their fading foliage disguised by emerging tufts of grass. Amazingly, this garden style is low-maintenance. Neither perennials, chosen for summer leaves and winter flowerheads, nor waving plumes of grasses (pale golden and buff in autumn) are cut down until early spring.

Margery Fish, author of many gardening books in which the character of cottage garden plants and their cultivation are described, made her garden at East Lambrook in Somerset just after the 1939-45 war. She gardened there until her death in 1969. The garden, which remains a model for her disciples, reflects both her passionate interest in individual plants and her rare instinct for plant association.

Round the walls of her old Hamstone manor house, she built up a network of beds densely packed with rare forms of quite ordinary small plants. Each plant was visually 'set off' by its neighbours and was appropriately placed both botanically and horticulturally; she achieved a sense of order but avoided any feeling that planting was contrived. Garden areas were defined by different planting themes. In one sunny corner, she grew grey- and silver-leaved artemisias,

Anthemis, pinks and creeping spurges. In another, plants with remarkable foliage, hellebores, ferns, peltiphyllums, more moisture-tolerant euphorbias and New Zealand flax (*Phormium tenax*) were massed in an old dry ditch. The garden also featured common and uncommon daphnes, tall *Euphorbia wulfenii* 'Lambrook Gold', a wide range of cranesbill geraniums, polemoniums, species peonies and vincas.

The gardening style at East Lambrook owed everything to Margery Fish's unique understanding and close observation of her plants. She watched constantly for seedlings which showed some interesting variation from the norm (see pp. 18-21).

The garden has been restored recently by Mr and Mrs Andrew Norton. They have captured the essence of the relaxed style and re-established her plant collections, thanks to the generosity of many who still own plants originally from her nursery.

FAR LEFT and LEFT Behind the malthouse, there is a steep-sided primrose ditch, once fed by a stream, where, shaded by apple trees, the soil is damp enough for choice plants which require moisture throughout the year. Ferns, hellebores and *Peltiphyllum peltatum*, with pink flowers in spring and parasol-shaped leaves through the summer, thrive here with different forms of *Astrantia*. Masterwort, *Astrantia major*, has greenish-white flowers surrounded by a collar of greenish bracts. Growing by the old stone steps at one end of the ditch, blue and white forms of *Campanula latiloba*, *Geranium endressii* 'Wargrave Pink' and in the background *G. × thurstonianum*, small *Vaccinium* and primroses, contrast with the spiky leaves of *Iris orientalis*. Other low-growing plants, including creeping ivies with differently shaped and variegated leaves, cover the ground with their foliage.

ABOVE Mrs Fish loved plants with variegated leaves; a friend, Dr Hampton, gave her a pink rose with glossy leaves delightfully marked with cream. The rose is still in the garden; identification has proved difficult but it is thought to be a variegated form of a Dutch bred rose, *Rosa* 'Werschuren'. Here it is shown in happy association with the pinky-purple foliage of *Berberis thunbergii* 'Rose Glow' and the flowers of *Astrantia major*.

LONGSTOCK WATER GARDENS

At Longstock in the valley of the river Test in Hampshire, a remarkable water garden covers an area of 2 hectares (5 acres). Surrounded by tall conifers such as the swamp cypress, *Taxodium distichum*, the garden is hidden from the rest of the parkland and arboretum. Fed from the river, but with flow controlled by sluice gates, the surfaces of almost stationary water are partly covered by water lilies and other aquatics. Islands connected by bridges provide sites for trees and moisture-loving plants. True bog plants, requiring roots and crown in moisture, and plants needing damp soil in the growing season have been carefully provided for.

The Longstock gardens, laid out for the John Lewis Partnership in the middle of this century, are examples of aquatic and waterside gardening at its best. They were planted with large naturalistic drifts of primulas, irises, ferns and many other good perennials to shape the waters edges. As a gardening style, it needs high maintenance and constant aesthetic vigilance. This means adjusting relative scales as plants grow and involves a considerable understanding of their development and needs. Waterside plants, often with large sculptural leaves, have a phenomenally fast growth rate if soil is rich, outstripping and even destroying less vigorous neighbours. Too little upkeep or too much thinning and replanting quickly leads to the superb effects of separate flower and foliage groups becoming confused. As in all gardening practice, the most satisfying results are usually found where the number of different plant types in any particular setting is restricted. It is far better to arrange drifts of three contrasting plant shapes, such as rodgersias, *Iris* and *Astilbe*, than to have smaller patches of many different types.

ABOVE Here, yellow primulas, royal ferns, day-lilies and arching sedges fill the foreground but allow a glimpse across the water to a group of *Gunnera manicata* and a swamp cypress.

LEFT Flower colours alternate with expanses of textured foliage. Here, a drift of pink candelabra primulas lines the water's edge.

RIGHT In this sort of garden, it is important to build up a pictorial composition at every viewpoint. The central water lilies provide a focal point of light in the view across the water. Round the lake, decorative grasses and plants such as irises provide vertical contrast with broader-shaped foliage. The invasive *Glyceria maxima* 'Variegata' has arching leaves distinctly striped with creamy-yellow; at Longstock it is allowed to spread as foreground planting to the reflecting water and rafts of lilies.

THE FLOWER GARDEN & COLOUR BORDER

Planting Themes . Mixed Planting . Gertrude Jekyll's Style

The Border . Planting for Colour

Giverny . Hestercombe . Tintinhull

There are many ways of organizing the beds and borders in which most of the garden planting is done. With a structure already well planned and established, further plant additions become 'furnishings'; emphasis moves to plants which contribute flowers, fruit and foliage. The gardener can now concentrate on plants with more fleeting and ephemeral attributes, rather than those of good form and habit which are essential qualities in the initial planning stage.

If a bed or border is the only planting area in a garden, it is a mistake to attempt to make all of it show some bit of colour and interest at all seasons. Instead, concentrate on one definite part for each period of the year, allowing the other areas to appear quiet and green in the 'off season'. In a very small garden it is not possible to have more than one or two different planting themes; in the best small garden the owner will make the maximum use of the site by doing one sort of planting really well. A shady town garden can become an exotic jungle dominated by sculptural plant shapes and large-textured leaves. In a sunnier and more open site, a formal design of box-hedging establishes a firm theme inside which bulbs, annuals and perennials are framed, massed or grouped separately, or in some combination.

Most beds and borders look their best when framed against a dark background and set off by smooth green lawn. Yew hedges with dark sombre foliage are the traditional foil to bright summer colours but their greedy and invasive root system can interfere with the growth of many good perennials. If there is space, make a border about 3.5-4.25 metres (12-14 feet) wide and leave up to a metre (2-3 feet) at the back for a narrow path between the hedge and the edge of the bed. These are optimum widths; of course the sizes of beds and borders are adjusted to fit in with the overall scale of a garden and, incidentally, with the height of a hedge or wall which backs the planting area; the number of plants in each group and drift is correspondingly larger or smaller. Groups of plants shaped in triangles or in drifts which weave through a scheme are more successful than groups arranged in straight lines (see *Planting for Colour*, pp. 176-8) and it is not always best to make strict rules about planting the tallest plants at the back. The composition of a good border plan requires not only the eye of a painter to match and harmonize colours: the arrangement of plants, which instead of being on a flat canvas is on different planes, also requires an architectural approach. Each group, as well as contributing colour and enhancing neighbouring groups of flowers, also gives a structure in three dimensions, and affects the feeling of depth in the scheme; plants of varying heights cast shadows and reflect sunlight in different ways as the sun strikes the scheme at different angles through the day.

PREVIOUS PAGES: LEFT On the lower sunny terrace at Kerdalo in Brittany, flower borders are grouped round a central lawn. Backed by evergreen trees (which also provide wind protection from Atlantic gales) and a splendid variegated specimen of *Cornus controversa*, silver-leaved perennials, catmint, euphorbias and roses sprawl over stone edges enjoying the warm situation.

PREVIOUS PAGES: RIGHT Sweet peas in mixed colours are grown informally through other plants and shrubs in a border setting at Child Oxeford, Dorset. Miss Jekyll always encouraged the use of 'secondary' flowerers which performed later in the summer, training them over the stalks and decaying leaves of early summer perennials.

Beds in grass, which we term 'island beds', are designed differently. These beds or borders can be viewed from both sides and, accordingly, need both a 'front' and a 'back'. Sometimes plants (all of which grow to approximately the same height) are chosen to give a uniform massed effect; at other times taller plants are placed so that smaller plants beyond them are hidden from immediate view, from whichever side the spectator is looking. Island beds need careful siting; without being linked to their surroundings, they may appear to 'float'. Some low-growing plants at the front will 'tie' a bed into the lawn, terrace or other flat area in which it is placed. Strong evergreen shrubs will also help achieve this and may be used to give unity with more distant planting.

BELOW LEFT In Francis Cabot's garden at La Malbaie on the St Lawrence river, Quebec, poplars are exclamation marks terminating the view. On rising ground the richly planted perennial borders line a narrow grass path where levels are adjusted with shallow stone risers. A layer of thick snow protects the crowns of these hardy plants during the winter months.

BELOW In the cold climate of this same northern garden, there is a short growing season between spring and autumn frosts; traditional planting of hardy perennials will be more successful than the popular 'mixed' border, where shrubs are used to give extra form and structure. Quick-growing, vigorous herbaceous plants, such as delphiniums in different blues, meadow sweet

(*Filipendula ulmaria*), *Centaurea macrocephala* and day-lilies, have a glorious burst of bloom in July and August.

RIGHT At Royaumont in the Ile de France, fruit trees trained as espaliers and honeysuckles on wooden framed pillars line the grass paths in the kitchen garden. In the narrow beds bordering the lawn are annuals, such as pink and blue-flowered clary (*Salvia horminum*) and *S. patens*, which are grown from seed and planted out in early June, after the last frost.

FAR RIGHT At Barrington Court in Somerset an old rose garden was replanted as a garden with predominantly white, cream and pale tinted flowers. Annuals such as tobacco plants are grouped next to silvery and grey foliage in the central beds which are arranged symmetrically round a sundial. In the outer beds permanent planting of hardy perennials such as campanulas and astilbes gives more substance and bulk to the scheme.

The most usual planting schemes are what we now call 'mixed': ornamental trees, shrubs, perennials, biennials and annuals, tender bedding plants and seasonal bulbs are all arranged together so as to give a long season. Alternatively, the same sort of plant association can be concentrated for a burst of colour for any one month, or for spring, summer, autumn or winter. The traditional perennial border where only hardy perennials are grouped for summer performance seldom exists in modern gardens where overall space is restricted. Few owners today would care to copy Miss Jekyll, who, among her garden areas, had an autumn Michaelmas daisy border, a spring garden, a separate hidden corner for her own strain of Munstead primulas, a pink and grey summer border, and, of course, her famous 'colour' border which reached a peak through the three months of July, August and September. Most gardeners prefer a 'mixed' content theme where single specimens of trees, shrubs or some large architectural non-woody plants are firmly underplanted and interplanted with drifts of lower-growing complementary flowers or foliage. The primary aim is often a pictorial composition of plants carefully but casually arranged in association to look as much as possible as if they might be growing together in natural conditions. In many ways the ideas behind these sorts of border schemes overlap with the 'natural' emphasis of the previous chapter; this style of gardening calls not only for a degree of skill in aesthetic design, with particular attention to relative shapes and sizes, but also knowledge of plant needs and behaviour. It is vital to have some grasp of the conditions of the plants in their habitats as

well as a good understanding of the aspect and capabilities of the particular garden site.

What we have learned from the great gardeners and garden writers who have come before us, is to use all or any plant material which will best achieve the results we envisage, inside the very relevant proviso that the whole scheme, whether simple or complex, is within the range of our own particular garden circumstances. It is just as vital for a successful outcome to choose plant types which, with available labour, can be helped to perform well; too ambitious a scheme will lead to nothing being well done and all results only at a moderate level. Bulbs, which can be treated like annuals, and annuals themselves, often placed in the beds as bulb foliage dies down, need realistic treatment. Some bulbs need summer baking; these, generally speaking, tend to die out in the mixed border. Others, which are able to survive light shade in summer, are more adaptable and will often become naturalized in a well-maintained soil.

Most of us try to make all our garden areas perform for as much of the year as possible. Some subtle planting associations where bulbs and deciduous shrubs grow together can give an extended season. Small colourful anemones, scillas, chionodoxas and cyclamen thrive under the light shade of spring- or summer-flowering shrubs; tall stems of lilies will thrust upward through the spreading branches of low-growing shrubs; summer hyacinths, *Galtonia candicans*, can be planted between the rhizomes of sun-loving German iris. Daffodil bulbs can be grouped between crowns of hostas or *Hemerocallis* and emergent foliage quickly disguises the decaying daffodil leaves. Late-flowering perennial and annual climbers look their best clambering through the foliage of shrubs which flower in spring. The small-flowered species of *Clematis* or the *C. viticella* types, perennial or annual nasturtiums, and other annuals such as cobaeas, maurandias and morning glories will all drape woody bushes without causing damage. This sort of gardening is experimental and stimulating; companion planting will make or break garden effects and skill in choosing plants to grow together lies not only in having a good sense of colour harmony but in knowing which plants will grow in similar conditions and give of their best at the same season. Most importantly, the time factor plays an essential role, more so in a mixed planting scheme than in any other border arrangement.

Generally speaking, annuals (plants which on the whole lack quality in their form and look best not as individual specimens but when massed together) grow quickest, reaching their peak in flower or foliage performance after a few weeks of being placed in their positions. Shallow-rooting biennials can often be reared in nursery quarters and only placed in their flowering site in the second season where they then, like annuals, rapidly develop. But

ABOVE At Levens Hall in Cumbria most of the topiary shapes, in green- and golden-leaved yew and box, were first planted and clipped at the end of the 17th century. In beds surrounded by dwarf box hedging, spring bulbs and forget-me-nots start the season; during the summer months red salvias and golden marigolds contrast with the sombre greens of the evergreens to give the maximum possible contrast of colour hues. Tender standard fuchsias, cordylines and silver-leaved cinerarias are used as 'spot' plants to give height and additional interest. This sort of colourful planting is at least purposeful if rather garish.

RIGHT At the Château du Pontrancart in Normandy, perennial sedums, blue-purple centaureas and white-flowered valerian are a foil to the 'hot' colours of scarlet dahlias, yellow zinnias and orange-red *Cosmos*, which are planted to make an impact in a separate garden area. From a distance these glowing colours blend in the eye like a tapestry rather than keeping their distinct hues. When laying out a border or bed, groups of annuals and tender bedding plants are added each summer until the more permanent plants grow together.

LEFT At The Gables in Somerset all the planting is mixed; shrubs, shrub roses, perennials, annuals and bulbs grow in the flowerbeds throughout the garden as well as in the wood. Many plants will tolerate much more shade than we might expect. Mrs Beaumont likes to repeat plant and colour associations and by doing so prevents the garden planting from seeming haphazard; a repetition of themes in sun and in woodland gives a strong sense of design unity.

RIGHT ABOVE At Lytes Cary, in Somerset, a long border backed by a stone wall contains roses, purple-leaved smoke bush (*Cotinus coggygria* 'Royal Purple') and other shrubs that are grouped effectively with vigorous perennials such as hardy geraniums, *Lychnis*, catmint and *Alchemilla mollis*. The shrubs and rose bushes are the most permanent of the plants; the herbaceous perennials need regrouping and replanting every few years to keep the composition in balance.

RIGHT BELOW In Sir Simon Hornby's old garden near Pusey in Oxfordshire, the curving beds were filled with a mixture of shrub roses, biennials such as foxgloves, and useful foliage plants such as hostas, *Epimedium* and *Brunnera* which provide interest even when the flowers are over. The secret of successful border planning lies in thinking in three dimensions as well as considering the more pictorial qualities of any garden scene. Bulky and tall plants give structure and depth, casting shadows in the low valleys between them. This sort of gardening is often called 'cottage style' but there is nothing simple about its conception; it involves a high degree of sophisticated planning.

ABOVE At Bampton in Oxfordshire, The Countess of Munster designed a border where grey- and silvery-leaved plants were used as foils to flowers in pale pastel colours. Designed as a summer border, and for many years considered one of the most effective in England, it is no longer planted in the same style. Its conception owed something to Gertrude Jekyll's own Michaelmas daisy border at Munstead Wood in Surrey. There, planned as a September feature, Miss Jekyll planted groups of daisy-flowers in blue, pink and white underplanted with silvery Stachys and glaucous-leaved Dianthus.

biennials with deep tap roots resent this treatment: the useful ornamental thistles, onopordons, eryngiums, silybums and verbascums need to get well established during their first growing season. Honesty, forget-me-nots, foxgloves and evening primroses can all be moved to their spring-flowering positions in the previous autumn, preferably while warm weather and soil will help a plant reestablish its root system and encourage a further period of growth. Most perennials require a few growing seasons before they attain their full beauty, and most shrubs and trees need years rather than summers to develop their mature shape and form. Evergreens, which are the most useful architectural plants, are generally the slowest growers; they will not survive if closely surrounded with short-term planting designed for effects during the intervening seasons. Brooms and *Cistus*, and bushy silvery-leaved artemisias and senecios, are quick growers but do not live long, generally needing replacing within the first five years.

This style of gardening, where informality of planting becomes a theme inside a quite formal framework, is typical of Gertrude Jekyll's many border designs. Much of her teaching relating to this aspect of planting, as conveyed in her books, remains as fresh and useful today as when she inspired the late Victorians and Edwardians to break away from their regimented bedding schemes. Few of the gardens she designed remain in reasonable order, and at Munstead Wood, her own garden, only a faint flavour of her style can be traced. There, her nut-walk stretching north beyond a paved courtyard behind her house, was typical of her simple planting technique. An avenue of the filbert *Corylus maxima* was underplanted with her own strain of Munstead primrose and other spring-flowerers, hellebores, anemones and bulbs forming a dense carpet at the base of the nut trees. At Hestercombe (which has been recently restored, see pp. 186-7) her use of informal drifts of planting, inside Lutyens' elaborate stonework garden frame, is worth studying. On one of the terraces she planned a border based on plants with grey and silvery leaves. Lavenders and santolinas billow over edges and even cascade down walls in naturalistic fashion. Gertrude Jekyll was trained as an artist and was an experienced practical gardener; her taste and knowledge of plants and their needs ensured that, in her hands, informal planting inside the garden frame did not deteriorate into a purposeless jumble.

This sort of planting became the prototype for gardens such as Hidcote and Sissinghurst and has come to rival the 18th-century landscape as the most important English contribution to garden style. Other important gardens that follow this style are the smaller Tintinhull and Chilcombe, Athelhampton, Westwell Manor, and the more modern Abbots Ripton. Mountstewart in Northern Ireland and Crathes in Scotland are also superb examples of collaboration between architect and gardener.

ABOVE In a simple perennial border at Stitches Farm House, East Sussex, early summer flowerers put up a good performance in June. Pale pink oriental poppies are backed by dark delphiniums; *Stachys byzantina* and pink mossy saxifrage, with lady's mantle (*Alchemilla mollis*) seen in the background, are lower-growing. All these plants finish flowering by the end of the month although vigorous delphiniums will perform again in September if flowering stems are removed. The attractive grey-green leaves of lady's mantle will renew themselves within ten days of being cut back.

THE BORDER

Many think that the hardy herbaceous border was an invention of William Robinson and that Gertrude Jekyll took his theme and expanded and sophisticated it to produce her masterpieces of orchestrated colour. In fact this is not so; Shirley Hibberd, writing a little earlier than William Robinson, was firm in his encouragement of the use of fine perennials which, dying down after the growing season and remaining dormant throughout the winter, commenced regrowth with warmer spring weather.

Even when the craze for bedding-out annuals and the making of pictures as 'mosaiculture' was at its peak at the beginning of the second half of the 19th century, traditional herbaceous plants were still grown in the more functional areas. In the grand gardens these old favourites occupied the central portion of a large walled kitchen garden, in wide double borders often backed by espalier fruit. Their flowers were used for house decoration to supplement hot-house rarities and plants in pots. At Arley Hall in Cheshire long double herbaceous borders were included in plans for the new garden in 1846; this is the earliest English reference to borders being specifically designed for ornamental effects in a garden layout rather than as 'useful' planting areas. In the smaller rectory or suburban garden herbaceous plants, many of them contemporary introductions, continued to be grown.

Hibberd points out that 'the bedding system is an embellishment added to the garden while the herbaceous border is a necessary fundamental feature'. Indeed, the border remains a fundamental part of almost any garden layout but the truly herbaceous border, with no concessions to woody material, bulbs, self-seeding biennials and the occasional drift of interdependent and appropriate annuals, is seldom found. Even Gertrude Jekyll used dahlias and other tender bedding-out plants; she used drifts of annuals to bolster her colour themes and sank pots of lilies or hydrangeas in any available space so as to prolong the performance of her borders into late autumn. At Great Dixter today (see pp. 96-7) Christopher Lloyd digs up early flowering perennials and substitutes annuals for his middle and late summer display. Like Miss Jekyll, he has a nursery business and divides and sells the plants; she provided plants to implement many of the garden schemes she did for clients.

Gertrude Jekyll gave us many hints in manipulation of border plants, particularly when planting is mixed. She trained or led trailing *Gypsophila* and perennial sweet peas forward over the untidy leaves of early-flowering herbaceous specimens such as the oriental poppy and July-flowering delphiniums. She also pulled down the stems of the tall sunflower (*Helianthus salicifolius*), rudbeckias, dahlias and Michaelmas daisies and pegged them to cover areas of bare earth or decaying foliage. Sometimes she even removed flower stems in order to delay flowering; a practice equivalent to pinching out annuals to encourage bushy growth and flowering side shoots. This sort of gardening is not time-consuming – it takes only a few minutes – but it requires frequent attention to detail and some fiddly fingerwork is always necessary.

Borders of hardy perennials need meticulous arrangement and, after planting, will take several years to reach their peak. Unfortunately, after that the plants grow and spread at different rates and some need dividing or splitting every few years. Without permanent planting of shrubs and bulbs to get in the way, it is possible to do piecemeal sorting out of individual groups as necessary; less frequently all plants are taken out and stored in a nursery bed, and the border scheme is completely rearranged. In the latter case, the bed can be completely dug and enriched with organic fertilizers. If necessary, the soil is sterilized and treated for 'replant' disease with a chemical such as dazomet. This is imperative if roses or many other of the family *Rosaceae* have been grown over a long period. It is also true, especially in an old garden which may have endured some neglect, that perennial weeds can be as vigorous as desirable garden plants; the worst of these, bindweed (*Convolvulus* sp.), ground-elder (*Aegopodium podagraria*) and creeping buttercup (*Ranunculus repens*) are best controlled by the use of a soil sterilizer or by applications of herbicide over a whole growing season. Golden rod, some Michaelmas daisies and many *Lysimachia*, attractive in restrained and balanced groups, will become as invasive and difficult to eradicate as some of the more traditional weeds.

Perennial borders need staking; most of the taller herbaceous plants need some support. Much depends on the situation and the incidence of strong winds and turbulence. A general rule is that stakes

LEFT At Bramdean House near Winchester the wide herbaceous borders face each other across a grass path which is aligned with the handsome gates and sundial in the further garden. Most of the planting in the beds consists of single specimens rather than groups of one kind; the strong-growers spread rapidly and the planting relationships need constant readjustment. Tall biennials such as *Onopordum arabicum*, a tall thistle with silver foliage, give height. In early summer the flowers are mainly blue and magenta; later, yellows and warmer oranges predominate.

should reach about two-thirds of the expected height of the plants. Hazel twigs, bamboos and string, metal-linked supports or heavier dahlia stakes can all be used; obviously they should be as inconspicuous as possible. If plants are staked in May or early June the new foliage quickly covers stakes and string. These perennial borders cannot maintain a peak performance for more than three months, usually from mid-June until October. When their dying flower stems are removed many of the early flowering perennials throw up mounds of fresh foliage and some, such as catmint and delphiniums, will flower again towards the end of the season.

Some gardeners like to tidy and reorganize groups of herbaceous plants as soon as foliage starts to wither and die down. Robinson had firm views about the value of crisp buff, brown and golden-tinged leaves and stems of perennials which are decorative long after the first frosts. In his wild garden these would be left to the care of nature, at most cleared away the following spring. There is a further good reason for delaying. Some biennials ripen and shed their seeds late in autumn.

October is the time for planning garden strategy, and in particular for thinking how to use good plants which give simple effects with minimum work. Prolific self-seeding biennials, which are often just short-lived perennials, can play a major role in informal planting. Seedlings germinate where they fall and are allowed to flourish singly or in groups, giving the garden a faintly haphazard but refreshing atmosphere. Unwanted extra seedlings are easily removed after germination, leaving those which flower in the next season to flourish in the shelter of maturer plants.

LEFT White lupins soar above the silvery leaves of the hardy *Artemisia* 'Powis Castle' at Darley House in Derbyshire. Lupins flower in June but a good foliage plant such as the wormwood will hold a design together and be decorative almost all the year. When planning a mixed border it is always worth considering planting some evergreen shrubs for winter interest; the 'silvers' seldom look their best after severe frosts but, after trimming back, recover quickly in early summer.

RIGHT Sissinghurst is a 'garden for all seasons'; all schemes are carefully planned so that each of the compartments will offer colour and interest through much of the year. By late summer *Acanthus* is in flower and roses already have decorative hips. The hydrangea, *Hydrangea aspera villosa*, sedums and a graceful grass (*Pennisetum alopecuroides*) all have a long period of beauty. Foliage effects are often as important as flowers with a more fleeting season: the silver-leaved *Artemisia* is a foil to the leaves of a variegated *Iris pallida dalmatica* 'Aureovariegata', and drooping grasses; *Acanthus* leaves are sculptural all through the summer; and the leaves of *Rosa glauca* are pale pinkish grey from early spring.

BELOW Hardy perennials including mauve salvias, crimson *Lychnis*, day-lilies, pink delphiniums and *Echinops* with thistle-heads are grouped together in a wide bed. The *Salvia* and *Delphinium* spires give a vertical emphasis to relieve an overall flatness in effect. In building up one of these border pictures the consideration of plant form and habit is as important as planning colour harmonies and contrasts.

RIGHT At Arley Hall in Cheshire, the double herbaceous borders were planned as a decorative feature in the layout of a new garden in 1846; they are thought to be the earliest example of planting where groups of hardy perennials are considered for beauty *in situ* rather than being grown only in kitchen gardens for cutting. Fortunately the borders are still well maintained and are a fine example of good gardening techniques and colour planning. An old brick wall runs behind one of the borders providing space for climbers. On the opposite side a yew hedge makes a strong dark background; yew buttresses and topiary add formality.

PLANTING FOR COLOUR

Just as garden designs often include too many features, so beds and borders can seem to be an assemblage of distracting kaleidoscopic colours. Colour planning for harmonies of related hues or for complementary contrasts of flowers, foliage and fruit at definite periods and over a seasonal period of months is all important for the final garden effects.

A proliferation of unconnected and unrelated blobs of different shades and tints is distracting; garden colour like garden planning should enhance an over-all feeling of unity. As you look at a planting scheme or walk along a border, each association of neighbouring plant colour followed by a progression of new colour relationships should seem to be logical as well as aesthetically pleasing.

Harmonies of shared pigment colour follow natural laws and require no focal adjustment, while contrasts, used deliberately, accentuate colour differences and sharpen the senses. Related colours placed together are restful, while complementary colours, those which are as different as possible from each other, invoke a change of mood. The 'hot' colours from the yellow, orange and red section of the spectrum give a startling feeling of warmth and appear to be closer than they really are; 'cool' pale yellows, greens, blues and mauves recede and disappear into the misty blueness of the atmosphere making the garden beds seem further away. Colour theory, which establishes how colours alter and affect each other, becomes a grammar to be used instinctively by the garden planner.

Any discussion of garden colour schemes necessarily deals with associated plants; indeed colour, or the colour we perceive, does not exist in isolation. Colour is much more than the hues, shades or tints of the rainbow; the colours we see are effects created by shapes and density. Even without considering foliage colour and texture, a shrub will appear heavy or light according to how it holds its branches and leaves; evergreens such as *Ilex* or *Osmanthus* will be weighty and solid as if tied to the ground, while the fresh young leaves of robinias, *Cornus* and most deciduous shrubs will appear light and feathery. Colours also vary with sunlight and shade; and colour variation is found in the shadowed pattern of leaves on grass or paving as they flutter in a breeze. Even in the most formal gardening where evergreen hedges make strong geometric horizontal and vertical patterns, we notice how the colour of the leaves varies as light strikes them at different angles.

To plan a border entails appreciation of all these factors, and, above all, an awareness of how colours appear to change when placed together. Although garden planning involves colour rules, and its successful execution requires the skills of a painter choosing and positioning his pigments on a flat canvas, there is a difference. Even in the very smallest and narrowest border, planting takes place on different planes, creating valleys and casting shadows between the various groups of plants or individual specimens, and the results of planting are viewed from many different angles. Planning therefore becomes three-dimensional and colour association will influence and control distance and dimensions. Just as the principles of linear perspective can lengthen or shorten a vista and can be deliberately employed to deceive, so aerial perspective allows garden colour to control and influence distance and size.

Colours alter and affect each other according to the laws of simultaneous contrast. Neighbouring flowers or leaves become tinged with the complementary or opposite colour of each other's flowers and leaves. Thus if reds and blues are adjacent, the red becomes tinged with orange and the blue becomes more green. White flowers set among green leaves become tinged with pink, but set around with neutral grey foliage appear more brilliantly white. Pure reds and greens, complementary colours, set together make each colour appear more vivid; similarly pure blues and oranges, and violets and yellows, colours as different as possible from each other both in hue and in intensity, also become brighter. These are immediate impressions but if you see plant colours in succession rather than in one embrasive glance similar results are found.

The degree to which neighbouring colours influence one another will also depend on the relative area or mass of planting. From a distance even the largest blocks of flower or leaf colour will blend in the eye to give an impressionist picture, while seen from close to each colour remains distinct. Usually in a garden both effects have to be studied; a bed is seen at a distance across a lawn or

FAR LEFT At Saling Hall in Essex planting in the walled garden is formalized with architectural cypresses and low box hedges which act as a foil to very relaxed planting schemes. In the borders Hugh Johnson plants blue, white and yellow flowers, all cool colours, which blend in the eye. Here, *Salvia* 'Superba', blue-flowered *Campanula latifolia*, Iceberg roses and yellow evening primroses are grouped together.

LEFT Spikes of white valerian and grey-leaved *Stachys byzantina* contrast with rounded shapes of clipped box in this border at Veere in The Netherlands. In most planting schemes, pale flower colours are easier to use effectively than harsher 'hot' colours; the brighter eye-catching hues tend to distort and foreshorten distance.

from a house window, the same bed will often be viewed from very close quarters. Single tulips planted in a bed of forget-me-nots, or flowers in an alpine meadow blend their colours to give an overall effect. In the wide borders at Bramdean House (see p. 170), mainly composed of hardy perennials, planting is often of single specimens in order to get this 'pointillist' result. In the early part of the season blues, mauves and crimsons predominate; later yellows and oranges, sunset colours, from daisy-flowered *Compositae*, take over.

At Nymans in Sussex, two borders over 90 metres (almost a hundred yards) in length, face each other across a narrow grass path. Planting consists entirely of annuals, for flowering from June to October, planted in triangles of twenty-five or thirty to each group. These are only seen from very close quarters or as a long view down the length of the two borders. There is no strict colour scheme but on this scale the multi-hued flowers blend and fuse in the eye.

In 'colour' borders elsewhere, planting groups are of a more generous size and it is the effects of simultaneous contrast which are important. These effects can be determined by colour theory but, of course, none of the flower colours are of pure rainbow hue; rather, they are paler or darker versions or more muted 'grey' tones.

Blocks of plants of any one sort are often grouped in threes, fives, sevens or more and planted as triangles; colour of flower or foliage remains distinct when viewed from close to, and only begins to blend in the eye when seen from a distance. The larger the size of each group of any one plant, the more firmly and distinctly does its flower or foliage colour keep its identity.

FAR LEFT In the Fellows' garden of Clare College in Cambridge, some of the fine borders are planned for specific colour schemes and for definite times of seasonal 'bursts'. By August yellow achilleas, golden rod and rudbeckias are massed for effect, while another area will be much quieter having been at its best earlier in the season.

LEFT In another bed at Clare, under a Judas tree, warm pinks, reds and oranges in muted tones blend in the eye. Here, where curving beds backed by woodland flow out on to the smooth lawn, colour schemes are more relaxed.

BELOW At Filoli, an American National Trust property near San Francisco, the garden is very formal; clipped evergreens and stonework make a framework for beds of spring bulbs and tender bedding-out plants carefully arranged for definite colour effects. In the walled garden, tulip 'Palestrina' holds its flowers above the white *Chrysanthemum palydosum*. Instead of keeping colour blocks distinct, as when groups of one plant are arranged in juxtaposition, the colours blend in the eye to give a mixture of colour, which is much more restful. The house, framed by stately Californian live oaks (*Quercus agrifolia*), was built between 1915 and 1919; the gardens were laid out around it in the years following.

RIGHT In this garden at Leaming's Run in New Jersey, the hardy native swamp mallow, *Hibiscus moscheutos*, is surrounded by annuals: white-flowered *Cleome*, *Euphorbia marginata*, with attractive variegated and white flower bracts, and yellow zinnias. At the back a white morning glory is flowering.

RIGHT At the Priory, Kemerton, Mr Peter Healing has created a stunning summer composition, using scarlet and crimson flowers against a background of purple and bronze foliage and green yew hedging. Drawing on Gertrude Jekyll's theory of garden colour, he uses complementary reds and greens, two colours directly opposite each other on the spectral wheel, which become noticeably brighter in juxtaposition. Scarlet dahlias, red penstemons and the crimson stalks of ruby chard all look their best during the last few months of summer.

ABOVE In Christopher Lloyd's garden at Great Dixter, pink alstroemerias, bronze helianthus and scarlet *Lychnis chalcedonica* are separated by a drift of deep violet salvias and sword-like iris leaves. The strong flower hues, linked by orange highlights, are backed by a group of tall artichokes with sculptural silvery leaves. Silver and grey foliage makes all neighbouring plant colour glow more brightly – a device often used in English gardens to avoid a 'washed out' look.

ABOVE RIGHT In this flower border, at Constantine in south Cornwall, a patch of orange *Eschscholzia californica*, the annual Californian poppy, is seen in front of the violet-blue perennial *Geranium × magnificum*. Two colours which are not quite complementary have deliberately been used together to give impact. Both pure hues are 'hot' in effect; even the dark violet, so different from clear cool azure blue, gives an impression of sunlight and warmth.

GIVERNY

LEFT From the front door of the pink farmhouse at Giverny one can see the arches over which Monet trained rambling roses. Tall bright yellow *Helianthus* grow behind mauve Michaelmas daisies and orange annual nasturtiums sprawl across the path. In the restoration of the garden Monet's planting schemes have been faithfully followed; in one of his paintings this scene is portrayed as it was before he cut back the large over-hanging branches of yew.

RIGHT ABOVE Pale-coloured irises, wallflowers, pansies and yellow and red tulips underplanted with a ribbon of forget-me-nots flourish at Giverny in spring. In his garden Monet placed bands and groups of colour which, when used as pig-ment on a canvas, blended in the eye to give the effects he sought.

RIGHT BELOW Seen from the front door, waves of pansies are banked in front of the wallflowers and irises. Monet used perennials and annuals in profusion; plants were encouraged to grow in unplanned masses rather than be restrained by the geometry of the straight paths.

Although flowers in bold splashes of colour seem to be everywhere at the *Clos Normand*, Monet's farmhouse garden at Giverny, the garden is in fact typically French. It is organized in a firm grid system with paths running in straight lines, parallel or at right angles to the house walls and the boundary roads. His paintings were of the flowers and not of the garden as a setting or landscape; his interest was in portraying the subtle effects of changing light through a day or through a whole season, in sunlight or in rainclouds, rather than in capturing the whole garden scene as a picture.

In the beds near the house, spring daffodils were followed by tulips; wisterias and clematis clambered over metal trellis, lilacs flowered above irises and peonies. In the orchards, under Japanese cherries and apple trees, clusters of oriental poppies and roses embellished the grass. By June, bellflowers, delphiniums and aquilegias grew in equal profusion; later, dahlias, Michaelmas daisies and hollyhocks continued the flowering season. Everywhere annuals were planted between the perennials to ensure that there was always flower colour to capture on his canvas.

Monet made his water garden by shaping pools from the diverted waters of the Epte. Willows round the edge and white and mauve wisteria clambering over the railings of the Japanese bridge filtered sunlight and reflections, allowing him to paint his famous water lilies from dawn to dusk, capturing each subtle nuance of changing light.

Today Monet's house and garden are a museum; the garden, known to many through his paintings, has been restored for all to enjoy.

HESTERCOMBE

The gardens at Hestercombe in Somerset were designed and planted by Edwin Lutyens and Gertrude Jekyll before the 1914-18 war. It is considered by many the most successful garden of their years in partnership. Taking advantage of the sloping site, Lutyens constructed a series of terraces, on different levels, joined by grand stone steps. Raised walks permitted views to the Taunton Vale and Blackdown Hills to the south; a sunken central garden, the core of the plan, was closed in by a pergola, stretching across the width

of the garden, to give a sense of enclosure and privacy. The brilliance of the architectural layout, in which Lutyens made use of local 'rustic' stone, provided the perfect foil to Miss Jekyll's planting plans in which she developed her ideas for separate and sometimes seasonal 'colour' themes while using good foliage plants to soften lines of stonework.

Fortunately most of these plans, in her own hand, survive and the garden has been faithfully restored by Somerset County Council. One scheme was for a

raised border where grey and silvery-leaved plants drifted over the edges of walls and, planted in pockets in the dry walling, cascaded vertically to make a curtained backdrop to a lower border in a similar colour scheme. On the East Rill, she designed a bed where pale blue and yellow flowers gradually gave way to 'hot' oranges and scarlets. This planting resembles her own border at Munstead Wood. To the west she planted lilies, roses, campanulas and foxgloves, edged with saxifrages and glaucous-leaved pinks.

ABOVE An overall view from the balustrading just below the house shows how the elaborate stonework which forms the basic structure of The Plat is an essential part of Lutyens' design. The pergola closes in the view but vistas look out over the countryside on the east and west. Gertrude Jekyll edged the triangular beds in The Plat with her favourite *Bergenia*. Peonies, white lilies, pink china roses ('Natalie Nypels' has been used in the restoration) and delphiniums are the main plants. Borders under the terraces reflect the style of the planting in the beds on the higher level. In the foreground, a bed of grey-silver foliage drifts over the edge of the high wall, linking the colour scheme with the border below.

OPPOSITE LEFT No plan was found for the pergola planting area but Gertrude Jekyll's recommendations for climbers on pergolas are well documented elsewhere and have been adapted. New planting follows her style and, where possible, makes use of varieties and cultivars of plants which she would have known. The pergola, built in the local stone has a double row of square-shaped and round pillars alternating across the raised bank. The pillars are joined overhead by cross-beams of chestnut.

OPPOSITE RIGHT In the rose garden where silvery-leaved *Stachys byzantina* 'Silver Carpet', the non-flowering form of lamb's ears, sprawls out over the paving at the edge of the beds, lavender bushes and hostas provide extra textural interest.

TINTINHULL

ABOVE Golden and pink alstroe-merias (*Alstroemeria aurantiaca* and *A. ligtu* hybrids) are separated by the grassy foliage and pale yellow flow-ers of *Hemerocallis* 'Citrina'; these and other vigorous plants fall across a gravel path behind a yew hedge. The alstroemerias are hard to establish but once growing well become almost too invasive. In this garden colour planning is very self-conscious; it relieves the tension to see plants asserting themselves.

RIGHT The Eagle Court, the garden compartment nearest to the house, is enclosed by high walls. Here, blue- and yellow-flowering plants carry the planting scheme from spring until September when pink Japanese anemones, followed by nerines, put up a good show. In July and August (illustrated) the almost prostrate blue catmint (*Nepeta nervosa*), and a *Penstemon* flower below lime green tobacco plants and the species *Nicotiana langsdorfii* which has pale yellow trumpets. The hardy *Agapanthus* and regale lilies have just finished flowering, and *Artemisia* 'Powis Castle' makes a mound of silver.

Tintinhull House in Somerset was bought by Mrs Phyllis Reiss and her husband in 1933; it is now the property of the National Trust. Mrs Reiss had lived close to Hidcote in Gloucestershire and had much admired Lawrence Johnston's layout and planting (see pp. 15-17). The garden at Tintinhull, with tall mature evergreen trees to balance with the house, and some 17th-century brick walls, could be designed in compartments in the same style. She divided the garden up with yew hedges using paths and stone steps to link areas and adjust levels.

Inside these garden 'rooms' she design-ed flowerbeds and borders with definite colour schemes; although the tightly packed planting resembled that at Hidcote, Mrs Reiss's ideas of colour harmonies were different. Instead of a 'red' border she had a red, yellow and blue colour scheme where Frensham roses, yellow verbascums and dark blue delphiniums were grouped together. This border, some twenty-five years after her death, is now composed of red, yellow and cream flowers. Opposite this 'hot' border she planted pale-coloured pastel tints, enlivened by strong architectural grey-leaved plants, set along the front of the border in a formal rhythm, a scheme which is almost identical today. She often

used the same plants in different parts of the garden, particularly those with grey or striking architectural foliage, as she felt that making links between separate garden areas gave the garden a coherent unity. *Senecio* 'Sunshine', woody artemisias (*Artemisia* 'Powis Castle' which became available in the 1970s is planted today) and purple-leaved *Cotinus* were among her favourites. In another compartment her most famous border mainly contained shrubs with purple and golden foliage. Purple and bronze-leaved *Berberis* grew next to *Cornus alba* 'Spaethii'; crimson 'Rosemary Rose', bright blue veronicas and red lyrthrums all flowered in season. Now, glaucous-leaved *Berberis* and bronze-leaved elder and viburnums have toned down the extreme contrasts in this bed.

In the fountain garden white and tinted flowers flourish with silvery foliage plants against a background of dark green yew; beyond in another small garden area glaucous-leaved hostas, blue-flowered willow gentians and ajugas grow to make a carpet below the outstretched branches of a pair of Asian dogwoods, *Cornus controversa* 'Variegata'.

Tintinhull has a highly formal 'colour' pattern but informality in gardening techniques and plants prevents the garden appearing too carefully studied. Many biennials are allowed to self-seed in all the beds; the resultant almost haphazard grouping of plants such as honesty, foxgloves, angelica, evening primroses and forget-me-nots prevents the garden becoming too manicured.

LEFT A section of one of the red and yellow border schemes in the pool garden at Tintinhull. Planting in the garden is all mixed; shrubs, bush roses, tall perennials, biennials and annuals flourish together. Golden yellow achilleas, scarlet 'Frensham' roses and crimson tobacco plants are grouped together; early in the season dark purple tulips and scarlet oriental poppies occupy the same site.

ABOVE A view of the west border at Tintinhull showing yellow-flowered verbascums, seedheads of *Crambe cordifolia* which finished flowering in June, scarlet 'Frensham' roses and pale yellow day-lilies. The biennial thistle with metallic blue-grey foliage and flowers, *Eryngium giganteum*, usually known as 'Miss Willmott's ghost', is encouraged to seed in the bed and give the scheme an unplanned effect.

GARDENS
WITHIN GARDENS

Inner Gardens . Garden Rooms . Informal Garden Areas

Villa La Foce . A Château in Normandy

Chilcombe . A West London Garden

A garden may be large enough to be divided up into smaller areas, each one developing its own planting characteristics. These areas or 'garden rooms', although they should be united with the rest of the garden by a definite overall plan which gives a sense of unity and cohesion, may well be enjoyed as a series of pictorial compositions which are viewed separately. Even if the garden is not large enough to make separate 'rooms', there is often space for some sort of extra planting theme which can be quite distinct from the overall style. A woodland low-upkeep garden, without a trace of organized formality, might yet accommodate a separate sunny area reserved for regular beds of culinary herbs or perhaps a formal flower garden. This may be an extreme example of contrasting themes, yet it demonstrates how difficult it is to classify gardens. Sometimes the themes will consist of definite plant types such as perennials, alpines or roses; sometimes they are organized in definite colour schemes such as a white garden, a blue and grey garden, borders with Jekyllean harmonies of strong hot reds and oranges or pale pastel tints augmented by silvery leaves, or golden foliage areas where cream and pale yellow flowers and leaves give an impression of sunlight. Garden areas set aside for performance in definite seasons extend the range of choice.

Almost all the ideas for garden areas and garden features discussed in this book can be envisaged as themes for 'gardens within a garden', rather than either representing or setting a style for the whole composition. The most successful gardens are generally those where not too many different features are visible at any one time; a journey round even the smallest garden should be a gradual progression where different planting features appear not only in turn but seemingly in a logical sequence.

The Victorians developed a very eclectic taste in garden themes; a garden such as Biddulph Grange near Stoke-on-Trent laid out in the 1840s and 1850s included an embroidery parterre, an Egyptian court designed with sphinxes in stone and clipped yew, a garden for American plants, a rose garden, an herbaceous border, a dahlia walk, a stumpery of old roots, a completely secret Chinese garden complete with weeping trees and pagoda, as well as a separate arboretum and pinetum.

Arthur Smee created a garden at Wallington in Surrey in the 1860s with the idea of 'little spots of cultivated wilderness or of special cultivation . . . where they are least expected'. His 'rooms' included a croquet lawn, a pear walk, a fern glade and mossery, as well as inner gardens for separate genera such as *Saxifraga* and *Sedum*. Generally speaking, the more formal themes, such as parterres, borders and rose gardens, are by tradition and for convenience near the house, while informal, more natural features are discovered in the outer garden areas.

Traditionally, one garden compartment is often reserved entirely for a formal rose garden which, quite unrelated to any overall style of a garden, may have a firm geometric pattern. But sometimes it is not only roses that are isolated in this way: at Polesden Lacey, as well as an Edwardian rose garden, there are separate iris and peony gardens, each hidden behind tall hedges. There is even a vast rock garden area where specially prepared stratified rocks simulate the natural conditions loved and needed by alpine-type plants. At the Villa Noailles outside Grasse, tree peonies are massed inside a secret enclosure (see pp. 54-5). Sometimes formal features have been deliberately introduced in outer garden areas: the rose garden hidden in a dark wood at Cliveden in Buckinghamshire; a formally-patterned maze of clipped cherry-laurel on a steep bank in the woodland garden at Glendurgan in Cornwall; and a formal Italian garden laid out deep in the wilder garden at

PREVIOUS PAGES: LEFT AND RIGHT At Tintinhull the 18th-century west front is framed by a walled enclosure, closely related in scale to the classical façade. An axial path of diamond-shaped flagstones divides the garden into compartments, each of which is devoted to some specific plant or colour theme. Regal lilies in ornamental pots frame the front door of the house which faces down the stone path.

ABOVE At the Dower House at Boughton House Valerie Finnis (Lady Scott) used railway sleepers to build raised beds against the walls of the old kitchen garden. Facing south, alkaline soil and free drainage was provided for alpines and Mediterranean-type plants with silvery and aromatic leaves. In shade against the north-facing wall, compost with a low pH allows successful cultivation of acid-lovers.

ABOVE At Hazelby House in
Berkshire the garden has been
made since 1947. Mr and Mrs
M. J. Lane Fox created a formal
framework of geometric garden
areas with brick walls and hedges
of beech, hornbeam, yew and
Thuja. These separate gardens are
joined together by pathways of
brick, stone, gravel and lawn. Many
of the compartments have high
divisions, but low hedges within
often further accentuate planting
themes. Beds with crowded
planting are flanked by lawn and
brick, while tall pillars clothed with
climbers give further architectural
accents. A trellis gazebo set in the
high hedge frames the entrance to
another garden area where a statue
is silhouetted against the yew and a
quiet pool reflects light. In this
garden deliberately contrasting
themes provide visual and
emotional contrasts.

ABOVE The famous white garden is one of the many enclosures at Sissinghurst Castle created by Vita Sackville West and her husband Harold Nicolson. Yew hedges make a perfect sombre green background for silver and grey foliage and plants with white or creamy flowers. Stone and brick paths further divide this garden area up into blocks. White, particularly pure laundry-whites, are not easy to use in a garden and can produce glare; here drifts of 'off-white' petals and cloudy flower umbels blend gently with background leaves to make this garden 'room' cool and restful.

RIGHT The rose garden within a walled area at Polesden Lacey has elaborate rustic pergolas and beds edged with lavender, a scheme which dates to Edwardian times when this separate garden section was first laid out. Some of the old varieties such as 'Dorothy Perkins' and 'American Pillar' are still grown here. The walled garden is also further sub-divided into areas for peonies, irises and a collection of lavenders.

Longwood in Pennsylvania are all effective surprise elements in imaginative designing.

Sometimes these 'views' are contained within physical or visual 'barriers' such as hedges, walls, paths or a line of pleached trees; at other times a shrubbery or a patch of ground shaded by a tree, or perhaps just a stretch of lawn, give less formal divisions. A separate planting theme may be indicated by low hedging: evergreen dwarf box (*Buxus sempervirens* 'Suffruticosa'), santolinas, lavenders or low-growing perennials can be used to mark out a ground pattern and provide a frame for inner planting. An illusion of division can be given by any low-growing edging plant; getting the scale relationship of the border and inner planting right is the important thing.

In a small city garden London Pride (*Saxifraga × urbium*) or the white- or pink-flowered forms of mossy saxifrage (*S. moschata*) will make delightful ribbons of colour in full sun; clumps of the small catmint, *Nepeta nervosa*, a species which produces pale blue flower-spikes all summer, also does well and is less invasive than its taller cousins. For a larger garden, *N. × faassenii* and the larger *N.* 'Six Hills Giant' is as effective as bushy lavender and will still give a good performance after a severe winter. Cut to the base after flowering, these catmints not only form new mounds of soft blue-grey foliage, attractive for the whole summer, but produce arching flower-spikes again towards the end of a season. Christopher Lloyd uses a mauve-flowered Michaelmas daisy with a stocky shrubby habit for a low hedge. In shadier situations, use the evergreen *Chiastophyllum oppositifolium* with its nodding yellow flowers on 23-cm (9-inch) stems.

In whatever way these 'gardens within gardens' are created, their effect is to ensure that the whole garden area seems larger. To give an impression of continuity, the designer must visually link all the themes, whether they are structured formally or informally.

In a very small garden it may not be possible to have actual divisions between seasonal or planting themes. Instead, by giving emphasis to areas in sun or shade, or to separate leaf or flower colour compositions or some other change of planting, it is possible to impose a different 'mood'. Often sun and shade dominate two definite areas of even the smallest town garden. If the whole area is in sun (unlikely even in a south-facing town garden which will often be hemmed in by neighbouring walls) a few quick-growing plants, used judiciously, will cast shadows on their north side; a tree, a shrub or even a group of summer perennials of appropriate scale can be chosen to do this. In the sun, grey- and silver-leaved Mediterranean-type plants are as different as possible from those which thrive in the shady area: ferns and hostas under-planting glossy-leaved fatsias, camellias, *Garrya elliptica* and climbers such as ivies.

Separate garden 'rooms' were traditional in Italian Renaissance

layouts. In Great Britain our gardens, towards the end of the Tudor period and in Stuart times, were essentially composed of similar separate but linked garden compartments. William Lawson recommends a layout for the smaller manor house and larger farmstead in *A New Orchard and Garden* (1618). A rectangular garden, the width of the façade of the house but three times as long, is divided into six equal parts. Decorative topiary, espalier fruit trees, a knot garden and sections for vegetables are divided by hedges or fences. In shape, if not in scale, this plan can be adapted for a smaller city garden of today. The Renaissance garden rooms became the inspiration for Edwardian garden designers, and provided the English gardener with the greatest and most inspired opportunities for planting. In each area the plantsman's love of collecting has to be limited by a chosen theme; the open-air rooms, geometric and structured, provide the horizontal and vertical lines against and through which the casual flowing and rounded shapes of plants can freely cascade. Gertrude Jekyll and Lutyens worked together to perfect this ideal; their style can most readily be simplified and translated for schemes for smaller gardens, and is particularly suited to late 20th-century gardening practice.

GARDEN ROOMS

Classical Roman gardens and Italian gardens of the Renaissance were divided into a series of rooms, where some separate garden feature would be emphasized. By the end of the 15th century, different garden areas might feature a boxwood parterre, a *giardino segreto*, a water basin or grotto with attendant statue of Neptune, or even a theatre in 'green' where hedges were stage wings and statues became the actors. Few original layouts now remain, although the garden at Villa La Pietra, recreated in late 15th-century style in the early 1900s, was modelled on contemporary garden plans. Arranged in a series of 'green' rooms of clipped yew, cypress, box and ilex, with little attention given to more fleeting and ephemeral flowers, the garden reproduces the spirit of these influential designs (see p. 76).

Many Tudor and Jacobean gardens in this classical style were destroyed during the English Civil Wars and most of those that remained were swept away during the 18th-century English landscape period. The vast Victorian parterres and so-called Italianate layouts of the mid-19th century bore little relation in scale to the garden rooms of Italian origin. By the end of the century, designers working round smaller manor houses were better able to capture the spirit of intimacy and seclusion that hedged compartments gave to garden planning. Inside a quite severe architectural framework were opportunities to design and plant in different themes (see pp. 186-7). A formal parterre or reflecting pool in one area could co-exist with Robinsonian hardy plant borders or Jekyllean colour effects in separate enclosures, without destroying the feeling of unity which is so important if the garden is to be an architectural extension and frame for the house.

LEFT At Knightshayes Court in Devon the pool garden is enclosed in high yew hedges, clipped to resemble the battlements of a castle. Inside the 'room' planting is minimal; a circular pool reflects the weeping silver pear (*Pyrus salicifolia* 'Pendula'). Long shadows cast by the evening sun pattern the grass. The emphasis is on privacy and seclusion; arches cut in the hedging provide entrances but do not stress views to the Devon countryside below the wide hanging terraces of the Victorian house.

ABOVE At Hidcote, in the garden laid out by Lawrence Johnston in the years before the 1914-18 war, a series of hedges frames geometric compartments and long alleys. While Hidcote's enclosures seem Italian in origin, the longer alleys fringed with clipped hornbeam more closely resemble the style of French 17th-century gardens where vistas were cut through forest.

ABOVE In Lord de Ramsey's garden at Abbots Ripton distinct garden areas have been sensitively adapted to aspect. In addition, in front of a high brick wall, facing south-west, soil has been specially prepared for growing grey, silver and glaucous-foliaged plants which need effective sharp drainage. In East Anglia summers tend to be dry and hot, ideal conditions for these 'silvers'; a layer of grit prevents moisture (which would freeze in winter) gathering round the crowns of plants. A rose pergola frames the view down the border which is hidden from the rest of the garden by a tall hedge of *Cupressus glabra*, carefully positioned so that the long bed is not put in shade.

RIGHT In an informal garden in Cornwall, delightful mixed planting is seen in two distinct areas. In full sun in the foreground silver-leaved *Anthemis cupaniana* sprawls over low-walling and stone and brick paving. In the further planting area woodland foxgloves grow in the shade cast by a tall elder tree.

INFORMAL GARDEN AREAS

Not all 'gardens within gardens' are geometric compartments surrounded by tall or low hedging. Quite often an inner garden area is indicated by a change of mood in planting rather than by a formal or recognizable style. Open sunny areas are for sun-loving plants; some specially prepared flowerbeds with low retaining walls and ample drainage will further distinguish this sort of planting scheme from a woodland or shaded area where plants revel in cool and sometimes moist situations. Most gardens will have scope for a change of theme, where planting possibilities can be quite distinct. In some gardens, such as the Dower House at Boughton House (see p. 192), soil composition and textures have been specially prepared for plant requirements.

Inner areas can be separated quite informally from each other; the overall scale of a garden will determine what style of planting or other device can be utilized. A line of roses (see pp. 64-5) possibly reinforced by planting to hide the bare branching stems at ground-level, a mixed shrub or perennial border, or low planting of informal edging such as catmint, London pride or *Dianthus*, or spreading plants which make horizontal carpets, will all do the job in a relaxed way. Obviously a grass path or wider area of lawn will act as a division of themes. It is equally possible to use pergolas (see pp. 200-1), lines of trees or topiary arranged in a regular rhythm like an avenue, or pleached trees which make an aerial hedge, leaving open views between the bare boles into further garden areas. Distinct colour schemes in areas of a garden can also be skilfully employed to induce a particular mood which defines a different area.

ABOVE and RIGHT At The Priory, Kemerton, two garden areas are informally separated by a rose and vine-covered wooden pergola. In an upper part of the garden, a seat offers an inviting place to rest; here the theme of relaxed mixed planting is based on pale-coloured flowers. Surrounded by flowerbeds, the lawn and seat provide a quiet oasis in a garden with many different themes.

In an adjoining area, a pergola partially hides a view of the border (see p. 133) which is planted to give a peak performance in June. To the left a tall thistle, *Onopordum arabicum*, marks the end corner of the main border which is behind the yew hedge. At The Priory summer borders are designed in specific colour schemes and each area of the garden is linked by mown lawns which flow easily between each garden area.

VILLA LA FOCE

Villa La Foce lies on the west slopes of hills in southern Tuscany, not far from Siena. Marchesa Origo (the writer Iris Origo) and her husband Antonio came here in the 1920s and restored the villa, by then a derelict farmhouse. Reclaiming much of the inhospitable land for agriculture, they then laid out a Renaissance-style garden in front of the house in a series of walled and hedged compartments to suit the sloping site.

From the villa windows, there is a view across the valley to the chestnut-clad slopes of Monte Amiata and the square tower of Radicofani, which in the past controlled the pass to Rome and the south. The situation of the Villa and gardens at La Foce would have satisfied Alberti when, in his *De Re Aedificatoria* (1485), he writes: 'a site should overlook a city or plain . . . bounded by familiar mountains' and that in the foreground there should be 'a delicacy of gardens'.

The Marchesa's father was American, her mother Anglo-Irish, and much of her childhood was spent at the Medici Villa in Fiesole just outside Florence. The garden she has made at La Foce, with the help of the English architect, Cecil Pinsent, reflects these influences. It is divided into 'rooms' as in a classical Italian layout with wide box hedging and lemon trees in ornamental pots. The parts of the garden illustrated contain no secondary planting, but other compartments, where flowers and foliage are used to soften the straight lines of formal geometry, are distinctly English in style.

RIGHT This garden 'room', on the flat terrace level with the villa, is enclosed by walls and tall hedges of bay. This was the first part of the garden to be designed by Cecil Pinsent in the 1930s and it remains austerely Italian in conception. Apart from the central pool and fountain, the low box hedges, patterned in 15th-century style, are the only other decorative feature. From the windows of the villa, the strict geometry of the garden provides a striking contrast to the rolling Tuscan hills beyond.

LEFT On a higher terrace, where box hedges have grown wide and high in the last sixty years, a wisteria covers the roof of a sitting recess, which provides a welcome respite from the hot sun in summer months. A simple stone seat stands out against a curtain of blue flowers. Above the recess, a wisteria-clad pergola is glimpsed; this feature runs parallel to a formal rose garden terrace before winding round the contour of the hill to reach woodland, some 200 metres (650 feet) away.

At Pontrancart near Dieppe a kitchen garden, separated from the moat and lawns by a wall, was originally laid out on a formal grid system with each vegetable compartment edged with yew. Today the yew hedging makes a perfect background for flower borders, mainly planted with groups of annuals, designed to reach their peak in August and September. The 'rooms' are all planned in distinct but graduated colour schemes; in each one, annuals such as *Ageratum, Cosmos, Lavatera,* marigolds and zinnias in a particular colour range are reinforced by groups of appropriate perennials.

The colour and plant planning programme is prepared many months ahead; implementation of plans for the following year begins as the season ends and plants are thrown away and the soil dug and enriched. Annuals are sown and planted out with a definite flowering period in mind; perennials are cut back, pinched out or manipulated to ensure that they, too, perform at the required moment. This sort of gardening requires immense technical skill and a sure knowledge of plants' seasonal behaviour.

FAR LEFT A white-flowered summer border at the Château du Pontrancart is backed by yew hedging. Designed for a six-week period of flowering, the planting is mainly of summer bedding plants; annuals such as *Cleome* and antirrhinums flower for many weeks and dahlias continue to perform, if regularly dead-headed, until the first frosts. Low-growing clumps of silver-leaved stachys and ageratums, planted along the border front, hold the design together.

ABOVE An overall view taken in summer of the flower-garden rooms on the far side of the moat shows the trim layout of yew hedges and allows a glimpse of the distinctive colour schemes. These gardens are particularly interesting as it is rare to find a modern garden planned for a six week performance. In winter the yew hedging still looks attractive, as it dominates the geometric layout.

LEFT In one of the garden compartments zinnias, blending in colour groups ranging through pink, red and orange, make an impressive array. Zinnias have little individual 'flower' or 'foliage' quality but when massed in this way, against dark yew, they achieve unusual perfection.

CHILCOMBE

At Chilcombe in Dorset, John and Caryl Hubbard's garden lies on a descending south-facing slope, with Chesil Beach and the sea only 1.5 km (a mile) away. Sheltered terraces support inner gardens which are sub-divided by cross hedges and head-height walls, physical divisions enforcing different planting themes and styles which give the whole garden an atmosphere of secrecy and an element of surprise. At the same time repetitions of plant groups in many of these 'rooms' prove that plants can be variously used to enhance many different design themes.

The main garden below the house is a walled area divided into squares and rectangles; espalier fruit trees, trellis-work arbours for climbing roses and rampant honeysuckle, shrub roses, evergreen plants with shiny leaves, and paths edged with low hedges make up the geometric network. John Hubbard is an artist and his wife is also a distinguished figure in the world of art, so each of the garden compartments is continually reappraised as a pictorial composition. Each forms a complete garden in itself, a meaningful horizontal layout of paths and flowerbeds. Architectural features are sometimes of plant structure alone, at other times, they take the form of trellis or tripods for climbers; taller plants from other garden compartments provide a firm background. The planting style is deliberately casual; in many parts of the garden herbs and vegetables grow among ornamentals, and cottage garden plants are encouraged to seed and spread. A closer look will reveal many choice plants growing deceptively well in between the others; that they grow successfully where they have been placed emphasizes the Hubbards' gardening skills.

LEFT An overview of the garden showing wide countryside beyond the tight layout. The land slopes steeply below the house, with garden levels connected by steps.

BELOW In one of the rectangular enclosures, cross pathways are cobbled with stones brought from Chesil Beach. Tender blue and red-flowered salvias, which survive winters in the mild climate, Iceland poppies, lilies, flowering *Stachys byzantina* and espaliered apples give a cottage garden atmosphere.

RIGHT At the far end of the cobbled garden, a seat in shade against the wall marks the garden perimeter at its lowest point. This garden room is deliberately inward-looking, stressing the contrast with the sweeping countryside beyond.

A WEST LONDON GARDEN

LEFT In the Raworths' garden, *Thuja plicata* has been trained to make an arched entrance to a garden area where box edged beds are set in gravel. The arch is centred on a white gateway which divides this formal garden from communal grounds where mature trees give a country feeling.

RIGHT, ABOVE LEFT Looking back through the arch towards the house, four symmetrically-shaped beds are edged with low box, *Buxus sempervirens* 'Suffruticosa'; in the centre of each bed a box dome is clipped into a formal shape. Lavender bushes and silvery foliage give this garden area a Mediterranean atmosphere.

RIGHT, ABOVE RIGHT A white seat is starkly framed by dark foliage to contrast with the colourful planting in the border. These garden compartments have alternating schemes; relaxed planting techniques and choice plants in one area compare with austere and much more formal arrangements in another.

RIGHT The conservatory was built on the north side of the house and, in the summer, filled with flowers and foliage, it becomes another garden room. The Raworths use a greenhouse to rear tender plants, such as white-flowered *Solanum* and scented pelargoniums, which flower in this extra sitting-room. Here, tender ferns remain luxuriant through the winter months.

Interest quickens at the gates of Mr and Mrs Raworth's London garden near Twickenham bridge. Pleached limes, underplanted with a continuous hedge of well-cut privet, give a sense of trimness and purpose to the hidden garden inside. The front path is edged with rosemary and lavender; to the north side an old *Catalpa* marks the garden edge; on the south a variegated holly is clipped formally into a roundhead. The house itself is clothed to the eaves with wisteria, a glorious sight in May; at the base two evergreen magnolias (*Magnolia grandiflora*) flank the doorway. A graceful snowbell tree, *Styrax japonica*, spreads its fan-like branches as a focal point to a pathway which leads alongside the north wall of the house to reveal several garden compartments formally framed in yew, beech and *Thuja plicata*. A tall hedge of *Elaeagnus* provides a foliage background to musk roses; against the conservatory wall, variegated *Cotoneaster microphyllus* grows above variegated ivies.

This is a garden where plant form and shape dominate the design; strong outlines are used to complement exciting and imaginative planting. In one area tall, screening hedges conceal box bushes clipped in spirals and domes; *Santolina* is massed inside low box edges. In another, silvery-leaved plants set in gravel catch the sun's rays under an open pergola. Through an archway of *Thuja plicata* a further 'room' is divided into four neat beds all hedged with low box in which white lilies and lavender are planted.

Gardens to visit

The gardens listed below may all be visited by the general public; some are open on a regular basis; others only on specific days; a few may be visited by appointment only. Those prefixed by the letters NT belong to the National Trust in the UK or equivalent organizations elsewhere, who should be contacted for up-to-date information on opening times. For information on English gardens prefixed by the letters NGS, contact the National Gardens Scheme, Hatchlands Park, East Clandon, Guildford, Surrey GU4 7RT (01483 211535). The prefix APP indicates that gardens may be visited by appointment only, often at the discretion of the owner.

BELGIUM

APP Garden of Hearts and Labyrinth Garden, adjoining Van Buuren Museum, Brussels
NT Mrs van Roosmalen's garden, Rekem

EIRE

Anne's Grove, Co. Cork

ENGLAND

NGS Abbotsbury Gardens, Dorset
NGS Alderley Grange, Gloucestershire
NGS Arley Hall, near Knutsford, Cheshire
NGS Bampton Gardens, Oxfordshire
NGS Barnsley House, Gloucestershire
NGS/NT Barrington Court, Somerset
NGS Beaumont Road, Plymouth, Devon
NGS Blenheim Palace, Oxfordshire
NT Bowood, Wiltshire

NGS Bramdean House, Hampshire
NGS Brockenhurst Park, Hampshire
NGS Chilcombe House, Dorset
NGS Clare College, Cambridge
NGS Cobblers, Sussex
NGS Cornwell Manor, Oxfordshire
NGS Cranborne Manor, Dorset
NGS Darley House, Derbyshire
NGS Docwra's Manor, Cambridgeshire
    East Lambrook, Sussex
NGS Great Dixter, East Sussex
NGS/NT Grey's Court, Oxfordshire
NGS Hadspen House, Somerset
NT Hatfield House, Hertfordshire
NGS Hazelby Court, Berkshire
NGS Hestercombe House, Somerset
NGS/NT Hidcote Manor Garden, Gloucestershire
NT Howick Hall, Northumberland
NGS Jenkyn Place, Hampshire
NGS/NT Knightshayes Court, Devon
NGS Levens Hall, Cumbria
NGS Longstock Park Gardens, Hampshire
NGS/NT Lytes Carey Manor, Somerset
NGS Newby Hall, Ripon, North Yorkshire
NGS/NT Nymans, West Sussex
NGS Owl Cottage, Isle of Wight
NGS Parnham, Dorset
NGS/NT Polesden Lacey, Surrey
NGS Pusey House, Oxfordshire
NGS Saling Hall, Great Saling, Essex
NGS Sissinghurst Place Gardens, Kent
NGS The Dower House, Boughton House, Kettering, Northamptonshire
    The Gables, Stoke-sub-Hambdon, Somerset
NGS The Old Rectory, Farnborough, Somerset
NGS The Priory, Kemerton, Gloucestershire

NGS/NT Tintinhull House Garden, Somerset
    Tresco Abbey, Isles of Scilly
NGS Vann, Hambledon, Surrey

FRANCE

    Courances, near Paris
    Giverny, near Vernon
    Kerdalo, Brittany
APP La Chèvre d'Or, near Biot
    Villa Noailles, near Grasse
    Villandry, Touraine

ITALY

    Giardino dei Giusti, Verona
    Piccolomini Palace, Pienza
    The Botanic Garden of Padua
APP Villa La Gamberaia, Florence
APP Villa la Pietra, Florence

NETHERLANDS

    Canneman Island Garden, Neerlangbroek
    Mr & Mrs Dekker's garden, Veere
NT/APP Mr & Mrs de la Hayze's garden, Middelburg
NT/APP Mr & Mrs van Bennekom's garden, Domburg

SCOTLAND

    Glen garden, Crarae, Argyll

USA

    Blake House, Kensington, California
    Deerfield, Pennsylvania
NT Filoli, near San Francisco
    Leaming's Run, New Jersey
    Magnolia Plantation, near Charleston, S. Carolina
    Western Hills, California

Bibliography

I wish I could include all the books on gardening which have helped me since I began my interest in the 1950s. A list of books on plants, garden history, garden descriptions and garden techniques, all of which over the years have given me inspiration and opened my mind to some new aspect, would be too long. Instead, here is a short list of the books I have found most useful on specific garden design and style:

Brown, Jane *The English Garden In Our Time* Antique Collector's Club, Woodbridge, 1986

Crowe, Dame Sylvia *Garden Design* Country Life Ltd, London, 1958; Heurthside, Great Neck, New York, 1959

Elliott, Dr Brent *Victorian Gardens* Batsford, London, 1986; Timber Press, Portland, Oregon, 1986

Hobhouse, Penelope *The National Trust: A Book of Gardening* Pavilion, London, 1986; Little, Brown & Co. Inc., Boston, 1986

Jekyll, Gertrude *Colour Schemes For the Flower Garden* Country Life Ltd, London, 1908

Lloyd, Christopher *The Well-Tempered Garden* Collins, London, (rev. ed.) 1985; Random House, New York, 1985

Masson, Georgina *Italian Gardens* Thames & Hudson, London, 1961

The Oxford Companion to Gardens OUP, Oxford, 1986

Page, Russell *The Education of a Gardener* Collins, London, 1962; Random House, New York, 1985

Robinson, William, *The English Flower Garden* John Murray, London, (15th ed.) 1933

Shepherd and Jellicoe, *Italian Gardens of the Renaissance* Ernest Benn, London, 1925; Architectural, Stamford, Connecticut, 1966

Sitwell, Sir George, *On the Making of Gardens* Gerald Duckworth, London, 1909

Some books that have guided me on plants and plantsmanship have been mentioned in the text (see especially *Inspiration and Education*). My two essential works of reference are:

Bean, W.G., *Trees and Shrubs Hardy in the British Isles* (6 vols) John Murray, London, (8th ed.) 1970 to 1980

Thomas, Graham Stuart, *Perennial Garden Plants* Dent, London, 1976; 2nd rev. ed. 1982 (for the Royal Horticultural Society)

Index

LEFT Narcissi naturalized in long grass at
Westwell Manor, Oxfordshire

Editor: Alison Freegard
Art Editor: Caroline Hillier
Assistant editor: Gian Douglas Home
Picture Researcher: Anne Fraser
Design assistance: Anne Wilson, Claudine Meissner
Other editorial contributions: initial planning, Penny David and Susan Berry;
proofreading, Susan George; index, Douglas Matthews

Author's Acknowledgments

I would like to thank Frances Lincoln who invited me to write this book, and Penny
David who helped me initially to work out a structure for my ideas. It is stimulating
and educative to work with perfectionists. I am very grateful to the team at Frances
Lincoln for all their interest, help and skill. I wish to thank all the owners and
designers who have produced gardens of rare quality for allowing pictures of their
work to be included; they not only illustrate the text but are an inspiration to better
gardening in the future. I wish also to emphasize the book's dependence on a number
of modern garden photographers whose work seems to get better every season.

Photographic Acknowledgments

For kind cooperation in permitting their gardens to be photographed, Frances Lincoln
Ltd wish to thank:
Mrs Ruth Barclay, Gwen Beaumont, Mr John Cavanagh, Mr and the Hon. Mrs Peter
Healing, Mrs Hannah Hutchinson and Miss Sophie Leaning, The National Trust and
the Knightshayes Garden Trust, Mr and Mrs Andrew Norton, Jenny and Richard
Raworth and Mrs C.L. Sainty

Specially commissioned photography by Jacqui Hurst and Georges Lévêque

(L=left R=right T=top B=bottom O=owned by D=designed by)
Agence Photographique TOP/Robert César: 100, 113T
Heather Angel: 71R, 87, 93T&B, 104R, 110, 122, 123, 144/5, 170, 186L
Geoff Dann: 25 © 131
Arnaud Descat: 56R
Ken Druse: 53L&R (O & D: Victor Nelson), 77
Richard S. Duncan: 60L, 61
Inge Espen-Hansen: 141
Derek Fell: 36, 37, 45, 48L, 68, 78, 134, 152/3, 153, 181, 184
Valerie Finnis: 192, 198L
Niccolo Grassi: 34, 35

Rob Gray: 60R
Mick Hales: 6, 43, 44, 48/9, 160, 161
Jerry Harpur: Jacket front, endpapers, 72T, 90/1, 104L, 108/9, 111, 152TL&B, 148/9,
167T&B, 178, 179, 186, 187, 195
Marcus Harrison: 132
Marijke Heuff (Amsterdam): 1 (O & D: Mr & Mrs de la Hayze), 3 (O & Mrs
van Bennekom), 9, 12, 50/1 (O: Mr & Mrs Degyter), 66, 67, 74, 75, 79, 82 (O & D:
Mr & Mrs de Haes), 116/7, 120, 177 (O & D: Mr & Mrs Dekker), 193
Saxon Holt: 62T, BL&BR, 63, 83, 115T&B, 180
Pat Hunt: 72B, 206T
Jacqui Hurst:
© FLL: 13, 14, 20, 21T&B, 47, 64L&R, 65, 85, 106, 121, 133, 140BL, 150, 154, 155L&R,
166, 188T&B, 190, 196/7, 200, 201, 208, 209TL, TR&B
© FLL reproduced by permission of The National Trust and the Knightshayes Garden
Trust: Jacket back, 26LT, LB&R, 27, 28, 29T&B, 146/7
© JH: 10, 52, 97, 130, 172, 174/5, 185T&B
Ann Kelley: 86
Andrew Lawson: 4, 81R, 147, 216
Georges Lévêque: 11, 17, 32T&B © FLL, 33 © FLL, 38, 39, 40, 46, 54, 55, 56L, 69,
80L, 89, 92, 96, 98TL&TR, 99, 112, 113, 124, 125, 126, 127, 135, 136L, 139, 140T
© FLL &BR, 142, 143, 157, 158, 162 © FLL, 163, 165, 168, 173, 176, 183, 189T, 191,
197R, 204, 205L&R, 207
Polly Lyster: 206B
Peter Margonelli/courtesy House & Garden USA: 58, 59T&B
S & O Mathews Photography: 7, 169
Tania Midgley: 49, 189B
Natural Image/Liz Gibbons: 156B; Bob Gibbons: 159
Newby Hall Estate/Dominic Cooper: 42, 80R
Hugh Palmer: 18, 19, 73, 101, 103, 138, 164
Philippe Perdereau: 84, 174L
Clay Perry: 182R, 198/9
Photos Horticultural/Michael Warren: 57
James Pipkin: 16
Gary Rogers: 76B, 81L, 102, 105, 118T, 136/7, 182L
David Schilling: 8
Dino Scrimali: 202, 203
Ron Sutherland: 24, 151, 156T
Elizabeth Whiting & Associates/Karl-Dietrich Bühler: 15, 31, 88, 91R, 94L&R, 95, 98B,
114, 118B, 119, 128L&R, 129, 194
Tom Woodham: 107
Steven Wooster: 22, 23L&R